About the Author

Margrit Dahm grew up in Germany, spent her early adult life in Hong Kong, and then moved to London where she studied for her master's degree. She began writing poetry as a student and published two books of German poetry. Her later discovery of meditation inspired her poetry in English and two of her books being published. She has also published her autobiography. 'The Lockdown Diaries' was written during the long weeks and months of the COVID-19 crisis.

The Lockdown Diaries

Margrit Dahm

The Lockdown Diaries

Vanguard Press

VANGUARD PAPERBACK

© Copyright 2024
Margrit Dahm

The right of Margrit Dahm to be identified as author of
this work has been asserted by them in accordance with the
Copyright, Designs and Patents Act 1988.

All Rights Reserved

No reproduction, copy or transmission of this publication
may be made without written permission.
No paragraph of this publication may be reproduced,
copied or transmitted save with the written permission of the
publisher, or in accordance with the provisions
of the Copyright Act 1956 (as amended).

Any person who commits any unauthorised act in relation to
this publication may be liable to criminal
prosecution and civil claims for damages.

A CIP catalogue record for this title is
available from the British Library.

ISBN 978 1 83794 006 6

*Vanguard Press is an imprint of
Pegasus Elliot Mackenzie Publishers Ltd.*
www.pegasuspublishers.com

First Published in 2024

**Vanguard Press
Sheraton House Castle Park
Cambridge England**

Printed & Bound in Great Britain

25th March 2020

I am listening to the Mozart Requiem.

Listening to it now makes up for the lack of human contact which is imposed on us due to the 'lockdown', and words like 'self-isolation' and 'social distancing' have suddenly become part of our daily vocabulary. News about the new coronavirus has become a regular occurrence. People are confused and frightened, and this whole aspect of uncertainty makes them act in a frantic manner where 'panic-buying' has become a menace to those who just want to do their usual shopping. Shelves in the supermarkets are stripped bare, and online grocery shopping has become an impossibility as there are no delivery slots available. It's all fully booked well in advance.

I went for my first 'lockdown walk' in our private gardens yesterday which will be my daily exercise. According to government guidelines, we are allowed to go for walks, apart from going to the supermarket or to the pharmacy. Here, in the gardens, I can take my time in the tranquillity of its green lawns and old trees. I might even meet a familiar face and stop for a chat, always keeping, however, two metres apart from each other.

I tried to order my repeat prescription by phoning the surgery and, after so many years of having collected my medication without any hassle at all, I was now told that I am not due yet for another prescription. I tried to explain that I always order it a bit early so as not to run out of any of it and, after a lot of discussion, I was finally told that I can collect it from the pharmacy in three days' time. I put down the receiver and realised that people even try to stock up on medicines as if we were facing a long-term siege. But it is a warm and sunny day, and the sunshine helps to keep everything in perspective. Bravely, with a sense of defiance, I say to myself: this, too, will pass and things will return to normal. But will they? And, if so, when?

26th March

Looking on the Bright Side

The coronavirus has hit us hard:
all of us are firmly barred
from all social and pastime fun,
worried and anxious is everyone.

But let us unite in our common aim
knowing that the world is not the same
as it once used to be
before the age of technology.

Now it's up to humanity
to recognise its destiny
where for the sake of the greater good
we begin to practice true brotherhood,

where none of us has to stand alone,
where emails are sent or else the phone
may ring in order to convey
what everyone is keen to say:

together we will beat the threat,
together we will arrest the spread
of a disease that has cast us down
but gives also rise to hope in every town

27th March

When you wake up in the morning these days, things first appear to be just as they have always been—just another day.

But then, it strikes you: this is not another normal day. People are asked to stay at home whenever possible. There is this disease out there which claims more lives every day.

This morning, I received a call from the dry cleaners telling me that they are closing their doors as of today, would I please come and collect my laundry.

Normally, when you are in the supermarket and something is out of stock, you don't bother very much and either forget about it or replace it with something else.

But now, so many things are unavailable that it worries and alarms you.

I received a call from my family today: they are stuck in Africa and flights to the UK have been cancelled due to the new virus. But they are safe where they are, at least for the time being.

28th March

I went to the pharmacy yesterday—one of the places we are allowed to go to. It was good just to be out, to be among people. It seems to me that we are more aware of each other than we used to be when, before, everybody just hurried along to their destination.

But it is still somewhat strange to see people wearing face masks and some even wear plastic gloves. It stresses the point that we are dealing with a highly infectious disease.

We have had other epidemics. There was the Black Death during the Middle-Ages, and no cure was found to shorten its run. There was the Spanish flu at the end of the Great War. My grandmother was one of its victims. Smallpox and polio were once diseases we were afraid of. We were able to find a way to prevent them, and maybe this time, too, we will eventually find a preventative cure for it.

I think we can confidently say: never have we witnessed a disease that has so speedily spread throughout the entire world, where no place on earth is exempt and which threatens our whole way of life. What started in Wuhan in China has turned into a world catastrophe, and it will be our task to curb the threat of this devastating menace, unanimously.

Every continent, every country is up against the struggle with a virus that is brand new and has never occurred before. The whole planet groans under its onslaught. It makes every discord, every puny disagreement, yes, every war futile in the face of such a powerful enemy.

29th March

It is as though Nature is sending us the message to wake up to the fact that we are not isolated beings, that we are all connected.

We are given the chance to come to this realisation and, rather than periodically destroying each other by wars and other means, we should now unite our efforts in the battle against this ruthless invader which puts all humanity at risk.

Now is the time when a good dose of idealism could well replace mere utilitarianism, when our consumer society may finally wake up to the vital question: what is really essential to our wellbeing?

On a larger scale, this could imply that patriotism makes room for humanitarianism.

We are all in it together. None of us is immune to the virus, at least not yet. So, let us, therefore, stand together when we start to take our defence against it, and let us share our scientific findings, our experiences and, above all, mourn together for those who have so tragically fallen victim to this disease already.

Let us celebrate our humanity in the wake of such a calamity.

30th March

In times such as these, when our resilience is being tested to the limit, we ought to ask ourselves: what is it that I can learn from this?

With this crisis, as it has become so familiar around the world by now, we can see more clearly that what kicked in first was our survival instinct—let's make sure we have enough food in the larder, enough of everything to last for several weeks. First come, first served.

People became obsessed with getting enough shopping in without thinking of those who came behind them. Even toilet rolls were out of stock!

But, given time, something else is required of us. We are made to realise that we are always part of a community where we have to watch out for each other and help each other.

This means that we have to give up a smidgen of our ego impulse which always wants to come first. We step back and find pleasure again in the stillness of nature, the flower opening, the blossom unfolding. It also means greeting the odd stranger in the street and coming to regard ourselves and others as being part of God's creation.

31st March

Having lived so long on my own, my life hasn't changed that much during lockdown, except perhaps that I don't travel to the high street anymore and can't see any friends.

I still enjoy sitting at home and becoming aware of my surroundings: the birds singing and chirping, the ancient tree outside my window gradually getting ready for another spring, the pigeons gathering on the roof top of the church opposite, and the general feeling this gives us when one season is ending and another one beginning.

Winter and the long nights are behind us now.

My two daily meditations provide each day with a framework and make sure that each day is lived in a fresh and unique way.

Every day, something is renewed, and, for that, I am grateful because it lets me know that I am in touch with something deeper, something which can only be found below the surface.

Under these new circumstances, where we have to live in isolation and spend more time at home, this is indeed a blessing and helps me to stay focused and in good spirits.

1st April

Not to mind being in your own company and even enjoying it, is something that needs practice perhaps. Not everyone finds it easy, as we can hear from the news.

People who are so used to computers, iPhones and tablets may find it boring and uninspiring. They may shy away from a time of reflection or from a time when the tank can be filled again with a better kind of energy; in fact, some may find it difficult to be confronted with themselves and become negative as a result.

Perhaps we all have to realise that each one is at a different point in their life, maybe at a different stage of development, and we all have a long way to go before we can truly become the person we were meant to or wish to be.

Some people acquire a certain kind of self-knowledge and understanding which then makes it easier for them to live in peace with those around them.

Being at peace with oneself is the precondition for being at peace with others and, only then, can we also learn the difficult task to bear any unpleasant behaviour which we may encounter in our daily life.

3rd April

It is a strange sight and an unprecedented phenomenon to see all big cities and smaller towns, here and everywhere, empty and abandoned, void of all normal activity.

Shops, department stores, pubs, restaurants and cafés—wherever you look, all is closed, and all will be closed for a considerable time to come.

Busses are running, but empty.

In front of supermarkets and pharmacies are long queues observing the rule of keeping 'social distancing'.

I had two days where I felt tired and listless, and I wondered whether I experienced mild symptoms of the virus. I cannot be certain. It lasted for two days, and then I was back to my usual self.

It is indeed a strange time we are having at the moment, where compassion and selfish behaviour are both present in equal measure.

4th April

So far, more than a million people worldwide have been affected by this deadly virus. No definite number has been given yet as to how many have died, but it is something like two hundred thousand or two hundred and fifty thousand.

There has been one doctor and two nurses in the UK who have fallen victim to the disease so far. Italy is hardest hit, then France, then the UK.

In East London, an old unused hangar, a relic from the last war has been turned into a hospital. They called it the Nightingale.

It was ready within the short space of two weeks and four thousand beds have been made available in this way, as the NHS is already stretched to the limit to cope with the many admissions of COVID-19, and the number of patients needing oxygen treatment and the like is expected to rise in the coming weeks.

And, while all this is going on, we are celebrating Palm Sunday tomorrow.

But the churches are closed, and there won't be an Easter egg hunt for the children unless it takes place at home or in the garden. Those who miss going to church have the option to follow the mass or service online within the four walls of their home.

5th April

Yesterday, I experienced first-hand what it is like to go shopping these days. I had hoped to go to Boots and the supermarket nearby.

The queue in front of Boots was so long that I quickly gave up the idea of joining it and will do my shop online.

The queue in front of the supermarket was equally long; but a kind woman who was standing in front encouraged me to go in first because of my age and I was able to get some bread, milk and yoghurt.

I think we all begin to realise that our old way of life has disappeared and that we are in it for the long haul, where we have to reconsider what is indeed important and what has to be put aside for the time being.

It is interesting to observe that at times like these— just as it was during and after the Second World War— people can be there for one another at a time when help and support are needed in so many ways.

Those, for instance, who are shielding and who are not allowed to leave the house at all, depend on the support from neighbours a great deal in order to get their shopping in.

Times of hardship always appeal to the better part in us, and so we are prepared to lend a willing hand, to show mutual support, as well as understanding and kindness.

6th April

While spring is well on its way and the cherry blossom in our street is coming into bloom, the coronavirus is not showing any signs of weakening.

London is still the hardest hit, and the number of people dying of the disease is still increasing.

At the same time, the economy, here as anywhere in the world, is under a lot of strain, and I wonder whether the world will stand together in order to get it going again once all this is over.

Touching gestures of compassion can be heard on the news like the story of a postman who, on his daily round, left a bag of fruit, vegetables and a bunch of flowers for a lonely resident which was received with a grateful heart.

Twice now it was arranged that, on a Thursday night at eight p.m., people stepped out of their doors to clap and applaud the many doctors and nurses of the NHS who risk their life day after day, often working a long shift of ten hours to look after an increasing number of COVID-19 patients.

7th April

It is such a perfect warm and sunny day here in London and, as long as you are inside or in the garden down below, it is hard to conceive that there is a disease raging out there that can potentially kill you.

Prime Minister Boris Johnson is in intensive care at St. Thomas' Hospital and has received many get-well wishes, including those of President Trump.

He spent one night where it was touch and go and, were it not for the dedicated care he received from the nurses, he might not have pulled through.

When he finally felt better, he was full of praise for the care he had received, but also warned when he addressed the nation, not to take this virus lightly and to stick to the rules of the lockdown.

I spring-cleaned my apartment while I was listening to the daily press conference led by the government and the scientists, where we are given the latest in the development of the disease.

I can hear the children's voices in the garden, and, in this sunny weather, more residents come out of the surrounding houses to enjoy a break from being closed in at home.

8th April

Within forty-eight hours, the cherry trees have come out in full bloom. Their white blossom gives the street the look of a kind of palatial grandeur.

I wonder whether sitting here, in the peaceful atmosphere of the garden, gives me a false sense of security. It is indeed an oasis in the midst of uncertainty and isolation.

I also wonder what these days of constant trial are telling us. Values can be put into question or seen in their real perspective. Reality has shifted. Our usual addiction to mundane and materialistic desires has been put on hold.

I think I can say that, instead, we are becoming more aware again of the gift of life in and around us. We notice the mystery again which surrounds every season, every day and every hour.

I hope that this spirit, which is now alive among so many, will still be with us when the disease has hopefully left us.

By then, we might not remember these days in so intensive a way as we do now and yet, perhaps they will stay with us for a bit longer, pointing the way to a state of wholeness and sanity inside and out.

9th April

Thank God for the little Indian shop down the road. No queues here. It not only provides me with some exercise, but I can also stock up here what I need in terms of groceries.

The weather is such that I have abandoned my winter clothes and wear my new top which I bought before the lockdown started.

Most people in the street are keen to keep a certain distance away from you with the exception of the occasional person who, apparently, has never heard of 'social distancing'.

The number of dead is still rising and has reached now over seven thousand in England alone.

Italy seems to have finally reached a plateau and small shops are allowed to open again.

It is Good Friday tomorrow, and I have already tasted some Easter eggs that I bought in the Indian shop.

I feel like celebrating so as to offset the doom and gloom of the daily news.

10th April

It is Good Friday. I have listened to Brahms' Requiem which I sang when I was a student at the RHBNC. Perhaps, it is appropriate in times like these to reflect on the theme of death.

Mentally, we can comprehend the idea that we must die. But, in our hearts, we can't really imagine it and seem to stay younger for much longer.

Our feelings want to live and, while nature is concerned with rebirth and renewal, we may give it some thought that, though we are presently surrounded by a lethal illness, we should also celebrate life in all its variety and multiplicity.

And, of course, Good Friday is not only about death, but it also holds the promise of life and resurrection. It brings hope into our life.

For me, it holds the key to the door through which we will enter from this life to the next. Life does not simply die. It will continue in another form.

Therefore, let us pause for a moment to remember that, with this crisis, which is our lot for the time being, there is not only the manifestation of death, but also of life, and life in abundance.

12th April

Easter Sunday! Amidst all the fear and distress experienced by so many, we celebrate this day when death has been conquered.

We so easily forget this message when we only see the aspect of suffering and torment.

Pope Frances said when he addressed the nations today: God does not by-pass human suffering but passes through it. He also said that this is not the time for division, self-centredness or indifference.

It is much rather a time when the opportunity presents itself to leave all warfare behind and to focus our attention on reconciliation and dialogue in all those areas and those different parts of the world which are still being torn apart by hostilities.

Now, as we are face to face with the same adversary the world over, it is an opportune moment to reflect on what can be done to create a friendlier and more peaceful world.

13th April

Easter Sunday has come and gone. On Easter Monday, we got the sombre news that the death toll has reached more than ten thousand and, still, there is no sign of the deadly virus giving up its hold on us. The numbers continue to climb.

I had a stroke of luck and was able to secure a home delivery for tomorrow which saves me a walk to the Indian shop. For the first time since this lockdown began, I am able to stay at home and wait for the delivery man to arrive. I think they have now organised that certain slots are reserved for older people like myself so as to spare them the long queues. One lady, who was in the queue at nine o'clock in the morning, complained: "By the time I got inside, the shelves were half empty."

Many people who, because of the lockdown, don't go to the office but work from home, have switched to online grocery shopping, and supermarkets like Tesco has experienced an increased demand for home deliveries.

It was a real joy for me to be able to return to my online ordering and shared the good news with my family, who I haven't seen since Christmas.

No visitors, no going out—what is the world coming to? I don't think the world will ever be quite the same again once this ordeal is over. I think it will have a long-lasting effect on people and, together with the wearing of face coverings and social distancing—no hugging, please—we will have changed some of our habits for good. People's livelihoods will have changed, too, and some will have to start over.

14th April

Many people will find it quite a challenge, I am sure, to follow the instructions given by the government during this lockdown, especially those people who normally like to lead an active life.

Suddenly, there is no need to go anywhere, no permission to go out just for pleasure or amusement.

The only places allowed are the public parks, where one household may meet with another or else it has to be in your own back garden.

I never appreciated my daily practice of meditation more than right now. It does prevent me from feeling isolated, because I feel inwardly connected and it gives me a deeper sense of self.

In fact, it makes me see more clearly that we are indeed all connected and now, more than ever before.

Never has the world been shrinking at a faster rate than right now when it has practically turned into one big global nation which applies the same line of defence against the same kind of perpetrator in order to survive and, ultimately, to re-establish a new order.

16th April

This disease is like a stone that is thrown into the water, where it draws wider and wider circles until it finally submerges again in the river of life.

Meanwhile, however, we mourn the many dead who, because the illness is so contagious, cannot even have their loved ones by their bedside and cannot have the kind of funeral they would have wished them to have.

We are also thinking of the many who live in crammed conditions; the children who cannot just go out and play. The rate of domestic abuse has gone through the roof. The government is aware of all these problems and does what it can to alleviate the situation, but it is never quite enough for so many who are losing out because of the present situation.

Salaries are paid up to eighty percent for all those who, because of the pandemic, have lost their job temporarily. The economy as a whole lies in ruin.

The Prime Minister is an optimistic and encouraging voice among so much upheaval when he speaks in the daily press conference and says: "I know that Britain will bounce back once we get this virus under control."

17th April

A war veteran has made history. He promised his family that, with the help of his walking frame, he would walk a hundred laps in front of his house before his hundredth birthday and raise £1,000 for the NHS. A week later, he is still walking and, so far, has raised the incredible amount of £13 million.

Everybody continues to be full of praise for the NHS and the dedicated work they are doing under such trying circumstances, and this also includes the staff working in care homes where there have been so many deaths among the elderly residents.

And we hear how one farm is sending out boxes containing anything from vegetables to spaghetti to Easter eggs. They are meant to be collected by the nurses when, after a long and tiring shift, they are finally ready to go home.

Another bit of good news tells us how a lady at the age of one hundred and six recovered successfully from COVID-19 and was applauded when she left the hospital in a wheelchair.

So, among all the bad news, these stories of bravery and compassion give us a definite glimmer of hope and allow us to look forward to a time when all this has finally become history.

19th April

Feeling mentally alert and being strong and healthy in your body is, I think, a good defence against an intruder like the coronavirus. Any little success in the battle for survival is then greeted with great enthusiasm.

For me, being able to order my usual groceries online for two weeks running now has become such a welcome gift and I feel greatly relieved that I don't have to go out to do my shopping anymore and can stay at home as I should, according to the rules, in order to protect myself.

We seem to have reached the peak now in the number of cases and deaths, but we are told that the lockdown will continue to last for another three weeks at least.

To think that, not long ago, we had never heard of lockdown or even knew what it meant! Face coverings and social distancing will stay with us even longer, but we don't know for how much longer.

Germany is the first European country to have eased existing restrictions. They had the smallest number of deaths compared to the rest of Europe.

20th April

Many of us will have to relearn how we spend our time and what to spend our time on. During this lockdown, most of us spend the greatest part of the day and, in some cases, the entire day at home, without any distraction by way of social interaction. The phone will have to suffice.

Those of us who are used to depending on external stimuli will find what is required now almost impossible. The computer has become, for many, the replacement for this lack of contact with friends and family. Zoom meetings and video calls are growing at a rate we could not have imagined before.

Although this bit of modern technology has certainly its place in our society and can make up, to a certain extent, for non-existent get-togethers, it is good to remember that we still rely on a certain amount of resourcefulness to shape our days' activities.

Every day still requires a beginning and an end. Things we had forgotten to do will come in handy again. In my case, I have taken up crocheting again.

The reward for us will be that we experience a certain degree of satisfaction and achievement at the end of the day, which leaves us happier and more fulfilled.

21st April

But let's not forget that such a sedentary lifestyle can put a strain on relationships and, unless we are willing to respect each other's privacy and private space, it will give way to anger, frustration or resentment, and may even cause a breakup under the weight of so many negative emotions.

What is the answer to this dilemma? I think we are all called on to try not to let things get out of hand and to do our best to maintain a certain amount of restraint and a lot of good will.

In the end, it comes back to the same thing: less selfishness and more thinking of the wellbeing of your partner, your neighbour, your mother, your friend.

I have always found that an hour of honest physical work rids us of any lingering negative thoughts or emotions.

Young people like to go for a run. I prefer to spend some time cleaning my windows or my kitchen which gives me the benefit of an immediate result.

22ⁿᵈ April

Many people wonder whether this crisis, because we are all affected by it, regardless of station, age or culture, will be something that will benefit mankind in the long run.

Some say we needed it as a wake-up call. Will we learn more thoroughly how to respect and accept each other, different as we all are?

The work that is being done at the moment to protect oneself and others is more intense than it has ever been before.

We are indeed in touch with something good here; good forces are at work at present when we often forget our own suffering because we are focused on the person beside us.

It remains to be seen whether such an expansive attitude will be able to outlive the virus and prevent us from reverting to our secure and limited lives when all this has passed.

A true change in man requires some deep-rooted and clear realisation, a resolution of some sort. Otherwise, the so-called change will be short-lived.

24th April

A sense of invention is vital in a situation such as we have at present.

Even if our environment consists of a shortage of space and a larger number of people, we can still find a small corner, if not at home, perhaps in the garden or in the park where, away from any noise or agitation, we are allowed to be quiet and alone, be with ourselves.

This refreshes our spirits, and we will return to the usual daily hubbub with a better kind of energy. It is nourishment for the soul.

Solitude is not loneliness, but a state whereby we don't hanker for company, but are content with what is and where our inner being can breathe freely.

For me, it is this that makes for a happy equilibrium which is then affected less by outer circumstances.

The more people realise the importance of such a difference between being alone and being lonely, the better it will be for our society and the more people will feel free to help others because they have learnt to help themselves.

26ᵗʰ April

When you are in the safety of your home, you forget that going out is only allowed if you either go to the supermarket, to the pharmacy or else go out for exercising.

The handshake has been replaced by touching each other's elbow and, otherwise, everybody must be kept at a distance of two metres.

When you watch a film or a program on TV and see people chatting and embracing each other, you automatically think: not too close, please—it has already become second nature to us and will be with us for some time to come.

For the first time, Russia has been mentioned in the news.

Hospitals are already working at full capacity and long files of ambulances were stuck on the road waiting to be admitted.

It was said that it may take up to nine hours for them to reach the hospital.

27ᵗʰ April

When I do go out these days, I do so with a heightened sense of awareness.

I began to notice that people look at you again when they pass you by—something that had been lost in a big city like London. People seem to have time to have eyes and ears again.

They look, register and acknowledge. Some greet you with their eyes only, some give you a smile or actually say 'hello'.

It is a small but significant gesture which makes us more human and more humane.

What had formerly simply disappeared in the vortex of life, has now resurfaced and connects us in quite a subtle way.

Long may it continue! Small gestures like these can help humanity to rediscover its potentialities and reinvent itself in a more responsible way and, by doing so, we recreate a bond where the built-in egoism makes room for loving your neighbour.

28th April

President Trump has given the go-ahead for America to lift the lockdown in order to get the economy running again.

But, as the different states are at different stages in the development of the pandemic, he has allowed the various states to make their own decisions.

Big cities like New York and London are facing a new problem.

They have the gruesome task to find enough space to bury the dead. A woman was mentioned on the news whose husband died of cancer.

But the family was told that they were in a queue and had to wait for at least two weeks before the funeral could take place.

Queues have become a fact of life, whatever you do and wherever you go. There are so many unexpected situations to consider, so many facts that we didn't have to face before, and it takes great ingenuity to deal with them sensibly and efficiently.

29th April

When I sit in the sunshine in the garden, I am like a contented Cheshire cat that takes in eagerly everything going on around her.

I become aware of the different sounds: the rustling of the wind, a blackbird singing high up in one of the old trees, children playing on the lawn, the odd person sunbathing, young men doing their exercises...

I can see that the strong winds we have had put an end to the blossom. It has been swept away and is lying now in huge quantities on the paths and the lawn.

The chestnut tree is now in bloom, its beautifully formed candles whipping in the breeze.

And, all the while, when I am thus watching and listening with my senses, I feel a pool of silence deep inside.

I don't mind at all not having to go far afield, I don't even miss the busy high street. Old habits are being put aside and new ones are being formed, and I can see that they are not at all restrictive, but enriching.

New impressions are being created.

30th April

I don't think we should restrict ourselves to just having fun but should aim at finding enjoyment.

There is a subtle difference between the two. Fun is a kind of amusement that remains entirely on the surface. Enjoyment feeds the aspirations of our hearts, it is experienced and met with our whole being.

Why settle for superficiality when we can receive impressions which stay with us and, ultimately, make us happier? When we rejoice in being alive?

Very often, it is our negative emotions which stand in the way and create a blockage to any happy thought or feeling wanting to enter. People who like to hang on to them, keep the door tightly shut. Nothing new can enter. They call it their burden, their albatross when, in fact, all they have to do is to let go.

This, of course, excludes real problems which may come our way and need to be resolved; but real problems often awaken in us an attitude where we take up the challenge and it then helps us to find a solution, and this is especially important when we are faced with the number of restrictions as we have them right now.

1st May

The heavens have been smiling on us with a lot of fine weather, lots of sunshine and mild temperatures.

But the news, on the other hand, continues to be rather stark. They have now a more exact number of deaths that occurred in residential and care homes; it stands at the moment at one thousand deaths during the week before Easter, all of whom are victims of the coronavirus.

Schools should have reopened by now following the Easter break but remain closed except for the children whose parents are part of the essential workforce.

These days, the provision of assistance and practical support has many faces. So, we hear, for instance, that costume and fashion designers have volunteered to produce scrubs and protective equipment for nurses and doctors. One such company is the 'London Scrubbers'.

TV programs have been created to provide exercises, and educational programs are available so that children don't fall too far behind.

Just every sector of our society is somehow affected, locally as well as worldwide. The price of oil has fallen drastically because the demand for the motor and aircraft industry has plummeted. Everything is suspended waiting for a release to take place and asking the governments to intervene by giving further financial support.

2nd May

In the newspapers, COVID-19 is being discussed now in connection with the climate crisis.

It has been established that, around the globe, the air quality has improved tremendously due to the fact that there are far fewer cars on the roads and nearly all flights have been stalled.

So, one wonders what will the world look like once this health crisis has passed which, right now, dominates every nook and crevice?

Will we return to the same hectic lifestyle? Or will the building of more turbines and electric cars contribute to creating a new society?

I cannot help thinking though that what is necessary in order to create a brave new world, is a fundamental change in man where warfare of any kind becomes a thing of the past, where we learn to live with each other in peace, where we can respect each other and where, in future generations, the resources which are now spent on military efficiency can serve mankind in a better and environmentally friendly way.

Will this remain utopia, or will man indeed wake up to the fact that it is in our interest to live in a more peaceful world while embracing all worlds?

3rd May

'Stay home, protect the NHS and save lives' has become the slogan that we hear from the government again and again and which are always the last words of the Prime Minister when he speaks in a press conference from Downing Street

During these days of general abstinence, renunciation and sacrifice, most people follow the guidelines laid out for them by the government, except, of course, the troublemakers who seem to think that these rules don't apply to them.

They don't keep their distance and seem to act out of sheer self-interest. Incapable of fitting in and doing what everyone else does, they simply ignore any warning signs which are given to us in the fight against this deadly disease.

It is an uphill struggle.

Can we envisage a time when everybody cares enough to save our way of life? I want to say and think that it will be possible. Meanwhile, however, we have to carry the burden of those who fall by the wayside.

4th May

So many people have died, people of all ages, though the elderly seem to be particularly vulnerable to catching this virus.

For those who have experienced grief and loss, the question: "will life change because of this virus?" has already been answered. Their life has already changed, and they were themselves changed by the impact of their loss.

As for the rest of us who live in lockdown, we might want to think about the question: how will it all end?

We hear the pessimistic outlook when people say that things will only get worse, or we might adopt a more optimistic view where we regard this time as a challenge, where new actions are born every day and people find new ways of living with these restrictions.

If this is the case, those rules and regulations don't really govern us, but, rather, we govern them.

For this to happen, discipline and generosity of spirit are necessary.

5th May

I was sent a video on my computer: a gigantic, curved wall consisting of more than a thousand faces moving across the screen like a huge tapestry.

Then, it turns into a long band, a vast strip before it begins to form a wide circle, in the midst of which stands the tiny figure of the conductor.

They all sing from home to the tunes of 'Finlandia' (the choir is Finnish) and they are in perfect harmony.

It is a very moving representation of something that concerns us all. It speaks of the goodness in humanity which, no matter what, always filters through to touch the human spirit, which is never defeated and can be united when, like in this case, many individuals become one voice, one song.

Such an extraordinary piece of work wants to remind us that, with this latest experience around the globe, a new thinking, a new attitude is required of us where the pockets of small-mindedness which we all carry on our backs, has to give way to a new sense of expansion, where, with a sense of urgency, we loosen the strings that tie us down to our seemingly isolated little selves and where we begin to realise the close co-existence that we all share and where we all become brothers.

6th May

We all have different talents and faculties which we can bring to the table.

There are the doctors and nurses who put their lives at risk day after day while the disease lasts.

But there are also the women and their sewing skills who help clothe these doctors and nurses with whatever they have available, for as long as the PPE is hard to come by and not enough to go round.

There is the whisky maker who decided to produce sanitisers instead. There are the teachers who, with their TV programs, help the children to be entertained and instructed.

There are the choirs that have been organised online, and there is Captain Tom, the war veteran, who is still walking up and down in front of his house and who, by the time he was a hundred years old, had raised an incredible £33 million for the NHS.

The country has really pulled together, and we can say that the world is mobilising new energies, new testing facilities to produce a vaccine in order to defeat this disease. Different nations and their scientists are working together, and that is a very hopeful situation to be in.

7th May

Despite the efforts which are being made, there are many individuals who, when you talk to them, worry or complain about 'not having enough to do' or 'keeping occupied'. Mental health problems are on the rise during these days of lockdown.

But on the other hand, a person who has an active mind will find a way out of a difficult situation.

I have heard it said: "For the first time in a long time, I hear the birds again and observe nature unfolding in a new season."

Such people experience a new kind of awareness which brings them joy at the same time because they seem to have more time for the little things that cost nothing. Instead of going to the office, they might take a walk in the park while working from home.

They know how to keep body, mind and heart together and they discover that we don't only consist of a body, but also need the kind of food which keeps our spirits up and our aspirations alive.

8th May

Modern technology seems to me to be a two-edged sword.

On the one hand, it gives us the possibility that we can, during a time of absence as it is enforced on us at present, be in touch with loved ones and friends. We can see each other on the screen. We can create all kinds of benefits with the tools which are available to us.

But this is only the case provided we know how to use them responsibly.

It has been said that people are spending at least three and a half hours online every day. It is really up to us to choose how far we let the technological world impinge on our lives.

A surplus of use can have an impact on our attention span, and we become easily distracted. This, in turn, can diminish our capacity for any kind of creativity through which we can express ourselves as individuals and which seems especially important at a time like this when we spend so much time at home.

The media, however, can also turn against us in a more destructive way. Like the story of the American woman who has been blamed for having started COVID-19 in America by bringing it back from China. Though she tried her best to deny it and to be heard, she has to deal with all the hate mail which she is still receiving every day.

9th May

Yesterday's seventy-fifth anniversary of VE Day was suitably commemorated as far as present conditions allowed.

There were some street parties on the outskirts of London with the usual bunting, cakes and union flags. People could not resist the chance to get outdoors and celebrate with either family or friends.

The old film strips were shown on television displaying Churchill and the Royal family on the balcony, but also the enormous crowds of people getting together and dancing in the streets when it was announced that the war was finally over.

Nazi Germany was finally defeated. Perhaps, because we are again going through a serious crisis, even if it is of a different kind, these scenes are of special importance to us just now.

Though celebrations had to be low-key because we are faced with another, but invisible perpetrator, people were glad to leave all isolation behind for a little while and fondly remembered the significance of that day.

Some of the old veterans who are still alive were shown on television, and the Queen addressed the nation just as her father had done before her when the end of the war was declared.

10th May

The number of cases of COVID-19 is on the decline.

But we must also remember that, meanwhile, the death toll stands at thirty-one thousand five hundred in all settings, for example, hospitals, care homes and in the community.

What is so sinister about this new virus is its unpredictability. If you catch it, you may get away with mild or very mild symptoms, like a new cough, loss of taste and smell and generally feeling unwell, or you may have to be admitted to the hospital because you need a ventilator and are seriously sick and, finally, you may have such severe symptoms that they can lead to your death, the most common cause being organ failure. We can never tell in advance what will be the outcome of it.

That's why many people are sincerely scared and anxious, asking all the time: how long will this last? The Prime Minister is frequently asked: how long will this lockdown last?

But, of course, he can't put a date on it because the answer is simply: until we see a general improvement in the situation. Some predict that, even when the lockdown is eventually lifted, the world will never be quite the same again.

In the end, we can only be glad that we are safely at home and that a time will come when life will be somewhat more acceptable again. Until then, we have to be patient and wait for better days to come.

11th May

The Prime Minister has spoken to the nation and laid out his plan for the coming weeks and months, now that the number of infections and admissions to hospital have come down significantly.

He stressed the point that, thanks to our combined efforts, the NHS was very busy, but not overwhelmed by the number of patients and he also mentioned that the rate of infections, known as the R-number, has fallen below 1.0 when, before, it had nearly reached 2.0. It stands now at 0.6 or 0.7. It is a healthy situation to be in.

As of today, those of us who cannot work from home are allowed to return to work.

If all goes well, schools and shops may open as of the first of June, and restaurants, bars, pubs and cafés will follow in July.

But he also reserved the right to tighten the rule again should there be a rise in cases at any point. He gave this new phase in our recovery programme a new slogan:

"Stay alert, control the virus, save lives."

More outdoor activities are now allowed as well, and the country remains hopeful that this is the small beginning of a return to normality.

12th May

The novelty of such a changed way of life has worn off by now.

At first, we probably thought that it will all be over within a month or two. But we have now lived with the virus for two months and realise, especially after having heard the Prime Minister's plan and having listened to the scientists that we are in it for the long haul.

We know now that we must simply persevere.

Normality seems a long way off. Shops will still be closed. Going for a haircut or pedicure will be impossible until July at the earliest. Churches will still be closed and, for the majority of us, it still applies: stay home unless you have to go to the supermarket or the pharmacy.

There is one ray of hope though which matters for families: you can now go freely to the park as long as you are members of the same household which means that children can have some outlet, even though playgrounds are still closed.

13th May

It has indeed become a waiting game.

The numbers are gradually coming down, but though there are fewer of them, another six hundred people still die every day which brings the total of deaths to thirty-eight thousand five hundred by now. The number of deaths in the care homes alone stands at eight thousand.

It is still hard to imagine that the whole world is wrestling with this infectious disease.

Every big or small country has a share in this, and every country applies the same methods to tackle and, ultimately, conquer it.

And we are far from having recovered. Today, people returned to work if they had to, and the Underground was busier than it has been for weeks.

On some trains, it was impossible to keep to social distancing and they are, therefore, considering making the wearing of face coverings compulsory.

What will the world look like when it will finally be over? Or will it ever be over?

14th May

People who are returning to work are, above all, construction workers and estate agents in an attempt to get the economy going again.

During the last two months, we fell into recession, and this is not only the case in the UK but also in Europe and the rest of the world.

There is much speculation about what this could mean for the next few months or even the next few years. How will we be able to adjust to such different conditions?

The government has extended the furlough scheme for another six months, but the loss of jobs is unavoidable and unemployment rates will no doubt go up.

Some firms will have to close their doors for good, despite the support which the government has made available.

But, on the other hand, there are also a number of smaller businesses who, because of the support they are receiving, will be able to survive and see things through to the end.

15th May

Some scientists are of the opinion that COVID-19 will never leave us completely.

They compare it with HIV and the way we have learnt to live with it and found treatments for it. But, in the final analysis, such speculations are not really helpful.

It is, therefore, refreshing to hear that New Zealand has lifted the lockdown, and people were queuing through the night to be the first to get a haircut.

Today, Australia followed by easing its lockdown: pubs, restaurants and bars reopened but social distancing is strictly being observed. This implies that there are fewer customers to be served but it is a beginning.

In the Netherlands, they give us an example of how this may be achieved. Each table is cocooned in a glass or plastic dome and the food is served on long wooden planks put from the outside onto the tables.

This is a time when people, looking for solutions, use their imagination to come up with new ideas and new solutions.

16th May

There is a lot of anxiety among the population which, sadly, also includes children who worry about their lack of schooling, about their parents catching the virus and having to stay at home too much.

The government has the hard task to make it known that it will only take a further step towards the reduction of restrictions if and when it is safe.

The number of cases is steadily falling. We heard that this week, there were only three hundred and eighty-four deaths and ten thousand new cases in hospitals compared to thirteen thousand the previous week.

Testing is widely available now and so we know that, so far, a quarter of a million have tested positive. The search for a vaccine continues and there is positive news coming from Oxford.

London, which was the first to peak in this pandemic, is now the first to indicate a dramatic decline in cases.

It is obvious that staying at home and observing social distancing are proving to be effective and it has helped to bring the rate of infection, the R- number, down to 0.4 in London and 0.7—1.0 in the rest of the country. The lower this R- number remains below zero, the better it is.

17th May

It is Sunday. Time to reflect and ponder. Acceptance of a given situation that we cannot change is the prerequisite of an ordered life. Instead of saying: 'I am fed up with this,' becomes then: 'let's live through another day as best we can. Let's make the most of it.' Such an attitude does not foster negativity, but rather welcomes the day in front of us.

Very often, it is not the situation that is the burden, but we are the burden heaving under its weight. In such a state, we are blind to our environment, we do not see or hear what is around us but are imprisoned in our own thoughts and/or emotions.

No wonder, then, that people get depressed or highly irritated and blame any old thing or the government for their unhappiness. They do not want to live another day in lockdown. Generally speaking, children are usually better equipped to accept a given situation. They take it lightly and are ready to move forward.

We, as adults, can sometimes learn from them how to keep everything in a healthy balance, whereas what children often pick up from their elders is their negative state and their negative complaints. A person who has learnt to be ready to accept what is before their eyes, is usually much better at putting up with unfavourable conditions.

As the saying goes: what cannot be cured, must be endured.

19th May

Too many people are still dying. It was said yesterday that 'only' one hundred and sixty new deaths occurred.

But, today, we got the news that, in total, there are now forty-one thousand who died of the coronavirus, and, among those, there are eleven thousand who have died in care homes. That's nearly a quarter.

We are also getting an indication of how things are bearing up as far as the damage to the economy is concerned.

Unemployment is dangerously high. Compared to one million before the lockdown started, there are now over two million who are receiving Universal Credit – a payment provided by the Government to help with the cost of living.

But good news is coming from other European countries like Italy and France where shops have reopened. Social distancing is firmly in place and face masks are being worn for protection wherever you go.

What a strange world it has become where physical human contact has become an absolute no-no, where solitude is fast becoming second nature and where we have to hide our faces behind a mask!

20th May

Another day spent in lockdown. It is best to take one day at a time.

What if we lived each day as though it was the last one of our lives? Would we not make the most of it and appreciate each gesture whether we are the giver or the recipient? A smile at a passer-by, a kind word to a neighbour, really listening to the voice on the phone…

Every day, we are given the opportunity to live fully by contributing to the web of life which is taking place in and around us.

'Love your neighbour' starts with little acts of kindness which, in turn, lightens and brightens our own heart.

A comforting word spoken to someone who is in distress or a light-hearted gesture to the person in the queue in front of us can change someone's mood altogether because there is a human being who cares, and we all need that someone who cares enough to think of us and to feel with us.

The world would be a better place if we would forget about ourselves more often and share with others what we have to offer.

That, too, can be contagious!

21st May

Our life has certainly changed during these long weeks and months where we continuously lived in close proximity to death.

And there are many areas in our lives which had to be given up: no more 'shopping-therapy', no more meeting friends for a coffee or a meal; elderly parents or grandchildren cannot be visited…

These changed conditions which are imposed from outside and which we have to adhere to, can, if taken seriously, lead to a new aspect of our personality.

For, let's face it, even with so many restrictions and giving up things we have held dear in our life, we still have a good deal of poor habits, too, which manifest themselves in our day-to-day existence.

We are still quick to criticise someone because he does things differently from us, and we still react if someone steps on our toes.

A real change is always an increase in our capacity to love, and that cannot come about unless we are prepared to let ourselves be changed, first, from the outside and then, from the inside.

22nd May

There are far too many fears and worries around. Questions that nobody is able to answer yet are being asked all the time: about a second outbreak or a second wave. Should children of forms one and six be sent back to school in June?

In the daily press conference, the Secretary of State patiently points out, again and again, that phase two will only come into action if the numbers of cases continue to fall and social distancing is maintained.

It is quite obvious that extreme caution is being applied to the present situation, and the government is making it their priority to weigh up very prudently and carefully how far and how soon should restrictions be lifted.

Our nurses and doctors have received and are still receiving a lot of praise, and quite rightly so.

But perhaps our ministers and scientific advisers could occasionally be applauded, too, for doing their absolute best to keep us safe and to get on top of this disease at the same time.

Instead, it seems to be the case that they receive nothing but criticism, blame and mistrust.

23rd May

Right now, it just seems as if we have not learnt anything from this crisis at all. Where is the solidarity we set out to achieve?

It was said in the beginning that only the combined effort of the entire nation could ultimately defeat this intruder.

But now, people are beginning to fret and think that they can find someone to blame for everything they are being put through.

We are dealing here with an invisible threat that confuses people. They do not want to accept that, as we still find ourselves in a situation where all predictions about a possible outcome are futile, there is no one to blame, but we should look at ourselves and ask if we really live by the rules which were clearly set out from the beginning.

A lot of scientific research is going on behind the scenes and I would, therefore, say that we simply have to put our trust in their well-thought-out plan. And, if the rest of Europe, like Italy, Spain, Germany and France, are slowly coming alive again, so will we, given time.

Some worry about the fact that their holiday abroad will most likely not take place, and a new word has been created: 'staycation,' which means that parts of the UK will be their holiday destination. This is good news for the local hospitality industry—an aspect which is better not overlooked as tourists from other parts of the world will be few and far between this year.

24th May

Many parts of the world are beginning to reopen their beaches for domestic tourism.

The Channel Islands—we learnt yesterday—lifted all restrictions of the lockdown but haven't opened their borders yet.

It means that families were reunited, new additions to the family were embraced by their grandparents for the first time, and hugs were re-introduced by young and old.

We, here in England, are still a long way off before such freedom will become the norm again.

But the number of cases keeps on dropping so there is cause for optimism.

I think it is true to say, however, that social distancing and face masks are fast becoming a fact of life and, therefore, the conclusion is made: the world has changed.

If we accept this, the next question is: is it a change for the better? Will progress be progress for the right thing? Will this general shutdown be the inspiration for building a better-defined world?

Only future will tell.

26th May

The study of public opinion is quite enlightening. Take the simple story of someone who has a prominent position in the government and who, out of necessity and in an emergency, steps over the line and breaks one of the rules established because of COVID-19 where we are not allowed to travel freely between different counties.

When superficially examined, this can give rise to criticism and, because an illegal step has been taken, the person might even be asked to resign.

When hearing the whole story, however, and hearing the reasons which led up to such a step, it seems to make perfect sense. It seems justified. But, of course, the story does not remain in the private domain. The media, including the newspapers, get hold of it and soon, the story appears in a totally different light fed by all sorts of imagined truths.

Now the public enters the arena, first a few, then a few more and, because they shout loudly enough, it doesn't take long before everybody believes what they have heard or read.

And, so, public opinion is born, void of all authenticity or validation of the matter which, in the meantime, has been grossly misinterpreted. No one seems to have the good sense to feel empathy with the victim. He is forced to resign.

27th May

We finally got the good news that as of 15th June, non-essential shops will reopen their doors. In the meantime, they must make the necessary provisions making sure that social distancing is in place and hand sanitisers are available at the shop's entry.

But pubs, restaurants, cafés, bars, hairdressers and nail bars will still be closed. The fact that department stores and other retail shops are allowed to open tells us that the downward trend of COVID-19 cases continues, and it is as if you could almost hear the people sigh with relief when they realise that something like normal conditions are about to return.

As far as a treatment for the virus is concerned, there have been some promising developments.

A drug that was used to treat Ebola has proved to shorten the time of recovery by several days.

Experiments have also been made where the plasma of people who have had COVID-19 and have developed antibodies is now used to treat patients in hospital.

The search for a vaccine is ongoing but will take time.

28th May

The new scheme which the government has developed is up and running as of today. It is called 'test and trace'.

It means that someone who has got symptoms should book a test. If the test proves to be positive, he will receive a call from the government and be asked to self-isolate.

The NHS will then trace the people the infected person was in close contact with, and they will be asked to self-isolate as well.

The government hopes that, with this scheme, they will be able to lift lockdown conditions generally and focus more on localised outbreaks.

Health Secretary Matt Hancock was very optimistic about this new scheme and hopes that it will minimise infections.

He stressed that co-operation is strictly voluntary but can be made mandatory if it should become necessary.

29th May

Last night, which was a Thursday, we might have witnessed the last of the ten weeks of 'clap for the carers and nurses' at eight p.m.

The woman who came up with the idea thought that it was time to stop, whereas frontline workers said that they felt really inspired by the weekly gesture.

There are now eight thousand patients with COVID-19 in hospital compared to eleven thousand two weeks ago. The daily death rate hovers between three hundred and four hundred. Testing facilities are now easily available, and this allows us to know that, so far, about two hundred and sixty thousand have tested positive.

People in England are now allowed to meet with six people from different households outdoors, be it in a park or a private garden.

It means that one could even have a barbecue at long last as long as people stay two metres apart from each other.

While such a small step toward normality is providing some happy relief, news of outbreaks of violence, like the riots in Hong Kong and incidents in Minneapolis, are a stark reminder that the world has not given up its aggression.

30th May

Oddly enough, flour is in high demand and, therefore, short in supply.

People have rediscovered the pleasure of baking during lockdown. Others are learning a new craft for which they had never had the time before.

Those are some of the more creative and imaginative options which provide a certain sense of satisfaction and some honest enjoyment.

But we also hear in the news that, particularly young people, are prone to depression and anxiety. Prospects of the future and their lack of them are often mentioned.

Lucky is the child or youngster who can turn to someone in the family who is able to listen with understanding, empathy and undivided attention, which has become a rare thing nowadays.

But it is the best way to detect what is ailing in a child and is waiting for an answer.

31st May

Today, Sunday, we celebrate Pentecost, the feast which, as a Christian country, we always associate with the theme of communication.

Once upon a time, so the Bible tells us, there was only one language among people until they began to build the Tower of Babel which was meant to reach into heaven. It was then that people lost their unification and began to speak in different tongues. They could not understand each other anymore.

But, at Pentecost, in the New Testament, the Spirit descended upon the apostles who were assembled in the Upper Room. It appeared as little tongues of flames above their heads, and they began to speak fearlessly to the crowds which had come from far and wide to the festivities in Jerusalem. While they talked, everybody understood them in their own language.

One may believe these stories and their symbolism or not, but we all know that we live in a world of division and separation, of fear and uncertainty.

With this virus, many of us have woken up to the fact that the present situation can no longer avoid the truth that we are all part of one and the same human race. At no time has it been more obvious that we are one human family and one world.

1st June

Nurseries and primary schools, form one and form six, are now allowed to receive pupils. They are back in the classrooms, much to the delight of the children who have missed their friends and their learning structure. Teachers made sure that social distancing is being observed, in the classrooms as well as outside.

We hear that about one-third of the parents were not convinced about the safety of their children and so were permitted not to send them back to school yet. But the Prime Minister said in his last press conference coming from Downing Street that it is of paramount importance that children should resume their school life as soon as possible so as not to delay their education any further.

Vulnerable people who have been shielding since March can now go out and meet with other people from different households. It must be a great relief for those who have not left the four walls of their homes for such a long time, that the thought of going outside is frightening for them at first.

Open-air markets are also in full swing again with their variety of stalls selling fruit and vegetable as well as clothing and household ware. But, here, again, the rule applies: always stand two metres apart from each other.

Horseracing has resumed, without any spectators though. The tribunes are empty.

It is true, however, that the rest of Europe is still far ahead of the UK as far as a return to a normal life is concerned.

2nd June

The world which has been aching under the impact of the pandemic for countless weeks and months, finally sighs with relief. Almost all countries the world over are easing some or most of the restrictions.

So, the Coliseum in Rome, for instance, is receiving tourists again. Italy and Spain are open for the tourist trade, and crowds of people are passing through the gates of the bazaars in the Middle East.

Here in the UK, we hear that hospital admissions are down to four hundred and seventy-nine compared to three thousand on the 2nd of April. Over the weekend, there were just a hundred deaths, the lowest figure since March.

Testing is widely practised. Over four million have been tested so far, of which two hundred and sixty thousand tested positive.

But we also hear in the news of the unrest and demonstrations taking place all over America after an incident had taken place where a black man, George Floyd, was killed because a policeman held him down too tightly, though he complained: 'I can't breathe'.

It has fired the whole question of racism in a big way. All rules about social distancing were quickly forgotten while people gathered to make their voices heard everywhere and around the world; a wave of strong emotion was set into motion.

3rd June

There are touching stories coming to light, like the story of a care home in Somerset where the entire staff decided not to go home in order to protect the residents. They have not seen their families for five weeks, with the result that all the residents are safe from the virus.

But, alongside these stories which speak of sacrifice and good will, there is also the news of how the tragic death of George Floyd has instigated large demonstrations in Minneapolis and other towns, and they have also spread to Europe and the UK, where participants are strongly rebelling against racial inequality.

London's Hyde Park was such a battle ground. The incident has incited a reaction just about everywhere, showing solidarity with the innocent victim.

Some of these demonstrations are peaceful and some turn into violence.

Any concerns about COVID-19 are pushed aside in these incidents, especially in the eyes of those who saw or heard of the unlawful killing brought about by the brutality of a policeman.

Underlying resentments are being aired which, especially in America, are still causing divisions among citizens.

4th June

As of next Monday, the 8th of June, the UK will introduce a quarantine lasting for fourteen days whenever you are arriving from abroad.

This has caused a lot of controversy, particularly among the aviation industry as they had hoped that the summer months would bring them some much-needed business.

BA and Easy Jet have said that they are obliged to lay off nearly one-third of their workforce. As time goes by, the real extent of the damage which the economy is facing worldwide is becoming more and more apparent.

The car industry is waiting for the time when restrictions are finally eased. Their sales have been practically down to zero during the last three months.

Chester Zoo might have to close down as the usual millions of spectators are absent, and London Zoo has got similar problems, above all, finding enough money simply to keep things going.

It is in times like these that it is good to hear someone speak about a future beyond the devastation of COVID-19, when countries will begin to recover. Such a voice is the Prime Minister right now when he addresses the nation with an air of optimism.

5th June

It is only becoming apparent now that many patients suffering from cancer or a stroke avoided going to the hospital to be treated because they didn't want to expose themselves to COVID-19.

Some treatments were postponed, but many simply did not come forward.

In countries like Mozambique or Southeast Asia, mothers did not take their babies to the clinic to get them vaccinated and, as a result, diseases like cholera, measles and typhoid are on the rise.

It is only now that we begin to see the full spectrum of complications as has been caused by the pandemic: economies having been destroyed, the health of many people put at risk, and no end yet to the general destruction it has caused.

What has become clear ever since I started to record the impact this disease has on our societies and people's response to it, is that nothing, absolutely nothing can be planned much in advance.

We have to move forward slowly and cautiously, yet persistently, and accept the 'new norm' as it is now spoken of and as is establishing itself worldwide.

6ᵗʰ June

I wonder how we will look back on this time of crisis when the whole world was laid low and suffered from the same disease.

Will it be one long, extraordinary incident in the development of the human race or the beginning of an age when something like this will occur more frequently as floods and heat waves have become more frequent because of climate change?

Much, I suppose, will depend on the progress we will make in finding an effective vaccine to combat these outbreaks in the future. There is also the question of whether this will help us in our endeavour to become greener.

Cycling, for instance, has increased significantly ever since this crisis began.

On the other hand, people are now quick to complain that they can't travel abroad and only some feel content to take instead a day trip to the green pastures and sandy beaches which this country has got to offer.

Discontentment and doubts about the regulations which the government feels obliged to make in order to stop the disease from spreading any further are the unavoidable reaction of our free society. There are those who are willing to live by the rules as they are given, and then there is always a minority who thinks that the government is wrong in inflicting all these restrictions on us, and finally, there are those who deny the gravity of the situation altogether, some going so far as saying that it is all a hoax.

7th June

How far have we really come to terms with all the outer and inner changes we had to accept in our lives?

Many of us, including myself, begin to grasp only now that these new regulations will be with us for a long time yet to come.

Maybe the hardest of them all is the fact that there is no more room for any spontaneous hug or embrace with family or friends.

The distance we have to keep from each other can easily create an inner distance as well and, for the time being, there is no cosy face-to-face or get-together while sipping a cup of tea in our sitting rooms as we are only allowed to meet outdoors.

But, as we stand all together when it comes to this new norm that has been accepted the world over, a positive element could consist of a new sense of direction for humanity which is accompanied by the common feeling of connectedness because, after all, we all share the same notions, the same experiences, the same struggle and, hopefully, the same recovery, too.

It really should unite us in a new way.

8th June

Today, the mandate came into effect that everybody who arrives in the UK has to fill in a form where they have to give an address which will allow them to self-isolate for two weeks. This new rule applies to British nationals as well.

Dentists who have been out of action for many months are slowly starting to operate again, but many are not ready yet because of the many safety measures they have to observe.

Children of forms one and six who are back in school were asked about their experience with the new measures as they were put in place before they returned.

Many said that they found it unfamiliar at first when they were welcomed with a hand sanitiser and had to follow the strict rules of a one-way system.

In the classroom, they no longer share a desk but have one each.

There are only ten children per classroom, and this 'bubble' stays together indoors as well as outdoors without mixing with other classes. Every so often, they are asked to wash their hands for twenty seconds.

But most of them were quick to say that it was good to be back in school.

9th June

A Sikh temple has been transformed into a community kitchen. They cook mainly chickpeas and lentils together with rice and thus provide the staff of the NHS or those in need with some nutritious meals.

Such acts of kindness seem to highlight the chasm between those who are ready to provide help and assistance wherever help is needed and those who simply continue following their own trend and ignoring others.

So, we have love and concern for others versus violence, indifference and criminality.

A touching story was told of a five-year-old boy who had lost both of his legs when he was a baby. Now, he has learned to walk on his artificial legs and, making the hundred-year-old veteran Captain Tom his hero, he pledged to raise money for the NHS by walking ten kilometres.

He just wanted to raise a modest amount of money. So far, he has raised more than £200,000.

The human spirit can assist us both to rise or fall, according to the desires and forces which drive us.

10th June

The rule of keeping two metres apart at all times—as essential as this is for the recovery process, while numbers of cases keep on falling—is causing widespread problems and obstacles.

Pubs and restaurants are already beginning to wonder whether it is worth their while to open at all.

The plan to receive more primary school children of different ages back in the classroom has already been abandoned because schools simply haven't got the space and capacity if this rule is applied.

Hospitals expect a large backlog of patients because of it. Dentists are struggling to treat enough of their patients.

And gone are the days when you could simply step into a shop or department store and leisurely look at the display of goods and merchandise, especially clothes, without feeling pressurised to keep moving by following the one-way system.

So many of us end up just quickly buying what we had come for and then leaving.

11th June

The whole country seems to be out of bounds. The field of gravity has shifted, and things lack their usual balance.

Many people are on edge as they had to give up their normal way of life, and that includes their work life which has become quite a precarious situation for so many, despite the generous schemes which the government has introduced to lighten the burden. People struggle and their complaints are many.

I wonder whether there is something in all this that we have got to come to realise in order to keep things on an even keel.

Everything points towards having to give up what we are accustomed to, something which is driven by some ego-orientated notion, and to replace it with something that is less conspicuous, but more useful at this time, and will serve us as well as others.

At this moment in time, it is relatively easy to see that we are not an isolated cell, but part of a nationwide as well as a worldwide community, whose immediate aim is to re-establish a balance that is morally, economically and culturally viable.

Surely, it is worth our while to make this effort, each in his own way and style. After all, we all depend on each other, more so now than ever before.

12th June

Apart from the non-essential shops, the places of worship, too, will be open again on Monday, but only for private prayer. For Christians, this means that things like the Sunday service or mass, and morning and evening prayer are only accessible online and on zoom which also means, of course, that they can receive communion in spirit only.

It will be a first step and a welcome change to be able to enter a church again and enjoy its solitude and restful atmosphere.

People who are inclined to put their trust in God and their faith know that this allows them to turn inwards and experience the kind of peace which transcends human activity. It gives them an additional strength that they would not have otherwise.

People who believe in divine love are found to be often more resilient in difficult situations and less prone to giving way to feelings of loneliness.

Hope comes into the equation and so they can better endure times of hardship by waiting patiently for the wheel to turn. This also applies to those who have discovered meditation as their daily discipline and practice. It gives them a sense of purpose, a feeling of self-worth and love for truth.

13ᵗʰ June

Old habits die hard—rather than continue to stand united when having to face this new enemy, there is clearly a voice of discontent and disunity in all sections of life by now.

The government has come under constant scrutiny when, for those who are watching the daily updates and press conferences from Downing Street, it is fairly obvious that scientists and politicians are trying their utmost to study, learn and cope, vis-à-vis this new and hitherto unknown virus.

But people are fed up and don't want to see that we are slowly moving in the right direction. Yes, of course, the economy has, as expected, suffered, yes, of course, people have lost their lives because of the severity of this virus, but so have other countries, not only in Europe but all over the world. No one is safe right now.

The unrest and demonstrations in the US and the UK since the tragic death of George Floyd have only added to this atmosphere of an antagonistic attitude toward the handling of the situation.

There again, it could be said: why not pause for a moment and also recognise how far we have come in our efforts to bring equal rights to all, irrespective of race or colour? There is always more room for improvement, of course.

14th June

A string of good habits goes a long way toward a happier life. They are the foundation of a life grounded in stability, equanimity and positive thinking. Once we have the right outlook in our own life, we can then help others who are still struggling.

So, what are these good habits?

Always look out for your neighbour and give him the esteem he expects and which you expect in return.

Stay on good terms with family and friends.

Avoid gossip and neither criticise nor judge anyone. Help the ones less fortunate than yourself, even if it is in some small way.

Protect your mind from too much clutter.

Be open to new impressions and new ideas. Stay inwardly alert and wakeful and never tire of working on your attention.

Don't ask for too much and be content with what is given to you.

If we follow these rules, we will create unison in ourselves which will then extend to others.

15th June

The brutal death of the black man, George Floyd, is causing wave after wave of outrage and rebellion.

We should, however, also keep in mind that many top positions in our society are now in the hands of black men and women, not only in politics, but also in television, in every aspect of public life, and also in the Christian church which welcomes people of all colours.

We all admire Mandela and the values he stood for. And there are many other examples that could be mentioned.

Prejudice is very often the result of ignorance on one side and of possible fear of the unfamiliar on the other. I myself had occasionally to endure prejudice against the Germans as this is the country where I was born and bred before I came to live in England, and when I was back in Germany on my visits, I met with prejudice against the English.

I knew, in both cases, that such preconceived ideas about people and countries existed because of a lack of practical knowledge about a given lifestyle.

These points of view I encountered, were usually expressed by those who were unfamiliar with either country. A society that has room for different people and their diverse cultures is the best background where we can learn to treat all people with respect.

16th June

As far as England is concerned, it looks as if we are halfway through the pandemic by now. With the reopening of retail shops, the high street is filling up with people again.

In Northern Ireland, shops are opening this coming Friday, and there is no definite date yet for Wales and Scotland.

Easy Jet has resumed some of the flights as of today, and some European countries like France and Germany are opening their borders. But flights to the UK mean that you still have to observe the fourteen-day quarantine until further notice.

There were only thirty-six deaths over the weekend, and the Prime Minister is considering easing the restrictions even further, above all, the contentious rule of keeping two metres apart, which may be reduced to one metre by the time cafés and restaurants or pubs are opening beginning of July.

People travelling on public transport have to wear the mandatory face covering as of today.

There is, however, the disquieting news coming from China, which, meanwhile, had managed to be free of

COVID-19 that there have been new cases, seventy-two in all, in Beijing.

17th June

The daily update and press conference about the coronavirus is like the sensitive needle of a seismograph that records the mood of the country.

Some fear that the restrictions are relaxed too soon, whereas, for others, they don't come off soon enough.

I tend to take the view that it is my job to listen carefully to the information, which is given every day by the ministers, as well as the scientists who are engaged in the study of the virus, and leave the tricky business of governing to the experts.

Indeed, the news that we are getting every day is somewhat grim.

The actual effects of a three-month lockdown are only gradually coming to light. Top of the list is the huge number of unemployed which is expected to rise even further.

Nine million people are currently on the furlough scheme which the government has created to help those who need help. Eighty percent of their salary is covered by this scheme. But how many will be able to go back to a job when this scheme comes to an end?

18th June

It is heart-breaking to hear some of the stories which relate how this outbreak of a deadly disease has destroyed some people's livelihood. We hear of young children who worry so much about possibly catching the virus that it has affected their inner balance and mental health.

The government is aware of all these problematic situations and does what it can to alleviate poverty and mental health issues.

But is it ever enough when faced with such a widespread problem?

The footballer, Marcus Rashford, wrote to the Prime Minister with the result that it has now been arranged that those children who need it will receive free meals throughout the summer vacation.

And there has been another piece of good news: the scientists who are always looking for a vaccine or treatment have discovered that the steroid Dexamethasone can prevent death in COVID-19 patients.

This is regarded as the first real breakthrough in finding an effective treatment that is inexpensive and widely available in all parts of the world.

19th June

The country has to find its way through so many difficult situations that arise because of this terrible virus which proves to be so hard to defeat.

People are still dying and, still, the death toll continues to rise again. The latest figure shows that two hundred and fifty-two died since yesterday, far too high a number to get complacent about it.

But far too many people continue to play the blaming game. Why blame the government when everybody, including most of the public, does what they can to get things under control?

We mustn't forget that we are dealing here with a disease that we had never heard of a few months ago. It's definitely a steep learning curve and that ought to be taken into consideration before we are blaming those who make the decisions.

Yes, we still need to have a quarantine in place where necessary, especially now that there are new cases in Beijing, China. We still need to keep our distance until such a time when, as in other European countries, the virus is firmly under control.

The country worst hit at present is Brazil, with the number of deaths completely out of control and it is still rising every day. Let's pull together and hope and pray that progress continues to be made.

20th June

People long for a return to normality, when face masks can be put aside and social distancing has become a thing of the past, when family and friends can come together again and children resume their lessons in school—in other words, when the fear of catching the disease is no more.

This 'new norm' which is imposed on us is anything but normal. So, we heard, for instance, that the Premier League has resumed their games, but they're taking place 'behind closed doors,' which means we can only watch them on the screen.

The same was true for Royal Ascot. For the first time in her reign of sixty-eight years, the Queen did not and could not attend, neither did anybody else.

Forms ten and twelve of the secondary schoolchildren have returned to the classroom, but there is much speculation about how it will be possible in September to fit all pupils in the space available if we want to stick to the rule of social distancing.

Modern technology like laptops, smartphones and TV have become more essential tools, in schools like anywhere else and, in that sense, they are a real blessing. But we also hear of young girls being groomed online and, sadly, as in so many other areas, there has been an increase since the lockdown began.

21ˢᵗ June

It has been announced that the alert level has been dropped from four to three. That means that the pandemic is still in circulation, but that the transmission rate R is below one. In fact, it is now 0.7 and 0.9.

There is also talk about the vaccine developed in the Imperial College undergoing tests, while the Oxford vaccine AstraZeneca is already being stocked in order to have it available, although, at first only for some vulnerable groups of people.

This is all good news and is certainly welcomed by everyone to bring a bit more hope into it all.

The cheering sight of seeing the high street populated again by shoppers is equally encouraging.

At last, we are able to step into our favourite stores again in order to have a look around or even get hold of a bargain, of which there are many at the moment because the shops want to make up for lost sales.

Thank God the picture of a ghost town has vanished, and people are coming out of their hideaways in droves.

23rd June

The social distance of two metres has been reduced to one metre to give pubs and restaurants a chance to make room for some more punters and have some healthy turnover at long last when they are allowed to open on the 4th of July.

There is a growing concern, however, that people who desperately want to return to their former lives with all its social implications, will be tempted to disregard the guidelines set by the government and do as they please.

Though things are being relaxed step by step, the scientists warn us that this pandemic is far from over. Apart from a new outbreak in China, there is America and Latin America, where over a million people are affected by the virus, and there is also India as well as hotspots in Africa, where the disease claims its toll day after day.

From Germany, we get the news that there has been an upsurge in one particular region and a local lockdown has been re-introduced.

Whenever restrictions are eased, as is the case in England at the moment, it is only too easy to forget that this dark cloud, which has been hanging over us now for what seems a really long time, has not disappeared nor has left us yet.

24th June

The Prime Minister gave one final press conference yesterday where he laid down the rules for the summer starting from 4th July.

He assured the public that it was now safe to ease and relax the restrictions further which will go down well with the public, especially the hospitality sector.

B&Bs and hotels will be able to open their doors for potential holidaymakers, and clubs, fitness centres, churches, bars, etcetera are all allowed to welcome back customers or parishioners respectively, provided a distance of one metre is being observed.

It's a great relief for all those businesses that have been closed for the last three months.

But, although the green light has been given to so many parts of our society, the medical adviser in charge warned that the threat of the virus has not gone and still exists and that we have to learn to live alongside it. 'We are in it for the long haul,' were his words.

Precautions have to be taken and we have to continue to apply great caution and great care.

25th June

We had our first picnic in the garden yesterday. My son and my daughter-in-law drove up from Leamington Spa and joined me for the first time since February.

We thoroughly enjoyed each other's company and the conversation never stopped. We laughed and joked a lot and just had a good time, grateful for being able to be together again, even if it had to be outdoors only.

This occasion gave me a chance to realise that the two of them were the first people I have seen in months and, therefore, to acknowledge the fact that, without ever complaining, I have been able to live through these days and weeks with a sense of inner calm and composure where loneliness was never experienced.

Instead, I felt that I was in touch with something in myself which is like a constant but invisible inner strength and which, like a companion, accompanies me in my daily activities.

It is such a convincing proof that a door is always open to us where we can experience the other side of us, which is so often forgotten, knowing that we are indeed not just flesh and blood, but spiritual beings, too, and the human spirit is one such manifestation of it in all its variety and multiplicity.

26th June

We are given the warning signs that this virus has not ceased to make itself known in a variety of ways.

In America, several states prove to have an ever-increasing number of cases. In Washington alone, the death toll stands at one hundred and twenty thousand victims, and it is said that, by October, there might be more than one hundred and eighty thousand.

And yet President Trump in the White House claims that the virus will go away, as he remarks: "There are far too many tests being carried out in America."

In Portugal, too, there has been an upsurge of cases in and around Lisbon.

But, at the same time, the UK is considering introducing 'air bridges' or corridors with other European countries, but a fourteen-day quarantine is still required if you return from any other country or continent.

Preparations are now underway to apply social distancing to cinemas but, as for the theatres, they remain tightly shut and some artists have taken the initiative to perform in any outdoor spaces they can find.

27th June

It was during the lockdown that I began to appreciate anew the beauty of our private gardens and to make full use of them. The weather played its part and gave us a lot of pleasantly warm and sunny days.

Today, however, London is sweltering in temperatures up to thirty-three and thirty-four degrees, the hottest day so far and, in such hot weather, many people flocked to the beaches on the South coast.

On some beaches, like Weston-Super-Mare, people seemed to be happy to stay apart from each other. But, on other beaches, any caution was thrown to the wind and the fear of another wave of infection is very real.

These trips to different locations in the UK are marked by the new attitude toward a holiday where the idea of going abroad has been abandoned. The Word 'staycation' has quickly become part of the English vocabulary.

For me, it means that I will spend many relaxing hours in the garden as there is always, despite the hot weather, a cooling breeze.

28th June

The Eiffel Tower in Paris has reopened after three months of closure.

Closer to home, however, the concern continues about a possible second spike of the disease.

There were more than half a million people on the beach in Bournemouth alone and, with such a large number of visitors, social distancing could no longer be maintained.

The Prime Minister spoke up and reminded everyone that the virus is still in circulation and urged people to act more responsibly.

There is the thought of limiting the number of people who are allowed to the Sussex coast if this weather continues.

It remains to be seen what will happen after the 4th of July, when Theme Parks and other entertainment venues open their doors.

Maybe this will even out somewhat the number of people who are travelling in and around the UK. We really ought to remember more often that we are far from a return to normal conditions. Perhaps, if we really did, we wouldn't have to face such complications.

29th June

It has now been confirmed that more than half a million have died from the coronavirus worldwide, the worst hit countries being America, with Texas and Florida in the forefront. Even though it has been said that people should wear face coverings, President Trump did not feel obliged to make it mandatory.

Here, in England, there is another spike of the illness reported in Leicester and the government has, therefore, imposed a local lockdown on the area which will last for two weeks, much to the dismay of shops and pubs who had hoped to be open for business at the end of the week.

In Wales, children have returned to school today and Scotland is opening its shops this week.

In England, however, everybody is anxiously awaiting the opening of all the hospitality and amusement sectors on Saturday and, at long last, people can book a hairdresser's appointment.

Air bridges between countries have now been established and, no doubt, people are looking forward to their usual holiday in countries like Spain or Greece.

30th June

The London Symphony Chorus has produced a piece of music where every individual voice can be heard. Their voices want to pay tribute to the many hospital and care workers who died because of COVID-19.

And there is the little five-year-old boy with his artificial legs we have mentioned before who wanted to raise £200 for the children's hospital by walking his mile on crutches.

It has now been announced that he raised over a million pounds, and he can finally have his well-deserved rest.

This time of unease and uncertainty seems to highlight the two sides of the spectrum when it comes to people's response to the situation.

There are those who act with real insight and compassion. Their spirit rests in the now and is ready to reach out. And there are those who remain untouched, thoughtless and quite selfish, and they come across as being careless and irresponsible.

Both make up our fragile and, yet resilient society.

1st July

Very moving stories come to the fore about patients who were admitted to hospital with COVID-19 and made an almost miraculous recovery after the family had already been told that the chances of survival were very slim.

And there are those who sadly did not make it and left behind a grieving family.

But it is also being said that, for the first time since March, the death rate has fallen to its normal level for this time of year.

In an optimistic tone of voice, we, therefore, hear the Prime Minister talk about his recovery plan for the post-COVID-19 period in Britain. He will be concentrating on improving the infrastructure of the country.

His slogan was: 'build, build, build'- build more homes, restore the NHS and focus on more and better school buildings.

He hopes that, in this way, he will create new jobs and more opportunities for business.

He reminded the public of the achievements that President Roosevelt accomplished when, through his efforts, he drew people out of the great depression at the time.

2nd July

The threat of job losses, however, has now become very real. It is known that redundancies are occurring in almost every sector of the economy.

Many retail shops are reducing their staff. Harrods is one of them. John Lewis says that it will not reopen all of their stores.

The aviation industry threatens with similar massive reductions among their staff: Airbus is laying off five thousand of their personnel, Easy Jet one thousand seven hundred and, all in all, they claim that it will take three years before the industry will be back to normal.

There is, meanwhile, also the threat of further local lockdowns like the one in Leicester where cases are still on the rise.

There is a general feeling of unease all around the country as people are worrying about what will happen when the retention scheme is coming to an end in October.

But we are not alone, and a downward trend was to be expected worldwide after three months of shutdown. So, let's try not to be too distraught and look to the future with a bit more confidence.

3rd July

There have been fifty thousand new cases of COVID-19 in a single day in America due to the fact that restrictions were lifted far too soon, and the President seems to think that it will all go away on its own accord.

As Leicester proved, the virus has certainly not gone away yet. Accordingly, the Prime Minister keeps repeating it like a mantra that defeating it must be the major concern before anything else.

There has been much concern about the children returning to school in September. The plan is to let each year form its own bubble. But do parents feel confident to send their children back to school?

Again, it will depend on whether or not we manage to keep the virus under control. The rule is: should there be one or two cases of COVID-19 in any of the proposed bubbles, the entire group will be sent home and asked to self-isolate.

On another note, it is planned to build an Emergency Services Memorial to honour the frontline workers and their constant effort. If enough money is raised, it will be set up in 2023.

4th July

Today, the big day has finally arrived when further restrictions come to an end and a sense of normality can return.

The hospitality industry is opening its doors again. New measures are being put in place to keep customers safe but are, nevertheless, invited to return to have their pint of beer, a cup of coffee or a meal in their favourite restaurant.

And let's not forget that everybody is eager to have their hair cut after a long three months when everybody's hairstyle had grown by several inches.

At the same time, a list of fifty countries is drawn up which allows people to travel abroad without having to face a fourteen-day quarantine after their return. America is not on that list as the virus is certainly not under control there yet.

And, though, for quite a while it was thought that Africa might get away lightly as far as the virus was concerned, it is now on the rampage in many parts of Africa, especially in the poorer areas.

Cape Town's hospitals cannot cope with the number of cases and not everyone can be saved. It is spreading like a wildfire.

5th July

There really was a celebratory mood among people on "Super Saturday": the first pint in three months put a smile on everyone's face.

Soho in London came to life again. Playgrounds welcomed back the children and, for those who wanted yet more adventure, there was the first ride in one of the theme parks.

People were able to enjoy themselves as the Prime Minister had promised when he announced the relaxing of so many more restrictions.

What a relief to be able to do what we used to do before the arrival of this pandemic and to feel halfway human again!

But we were also told by the experts as well as the Prime Minister in his press conference on Friday that, "we are not out of the woods yet".

Spikes can turn up at any time and in any place unless we continue to behave responsibly and sensibly.

He did mention, however, that he hopes to avoid any further national lockdowns and concentrate more on local outbreaks if necessary.

6th July

While England enjoyed its first taste of regained freedom, Wales follows foot and as of today, the restriction of being only allowed five miles from home is being lifted.

Two households can also meet indoors and stay overnight—these steps which are being taken are most important for the tourist industry.

In Scotland, people may gather in a beer garden or a pavement café. But shops will only open on 15th July.

Here, in England, people are now impatiently awaiting the dates which will be given when museums, galleries, music venues and theatres are all allowed to welcome back audiences.

Two and a half million pounds will be provided for the arts sector to make up for the loss during lockdown.

The NHS is celebrating its seventy third anniversary. However, it has now been revealed that, because of the pandemic, an excess of cancer deaths is likely to occur as treatments were put on hold for more than three months.

7th July

There is a mixed bag of news coming through today. Pubs in Somerset, Yorkshire and Hampshire had to close again when some of their customers tested positive for coronavirus.

Australia, too, was in the news. For the first time in a hundred years, the border between Victoria and South Wales was closed because of a new outbreak in Melbourne. One hundred and ninety-two people were reported ill in twenty-four hours.

It proves again that this virus is stubbornly lingering on wherever it can and does not give up its grip which it still has on us wherever we are.

We really must be extra careful in whatever we do, knowing that the threat is always there, lurking in the background.

On the other hand, we can't afford to be overly anxious and continue to do what we ought to be doing, remembering, however: be alert, control the virus and save lives.

It is a hard battle that can only be won if we all apply vigilance and keep on following the guidelines which are given to protect us.

8th July

While Wimbledon's tennis tournaments of past decades are being shown on TV in replacement of this year's games and cricket is resumed without an audience, the President of Brazil, who has repeatedly played down the danger of this disease, has tested positive and developed the typical symptoms of a fever and cough.

Brazil has seen sixty-five thousand deaths—the second highest rate, the US being the highest.

Back in England, we hear that those care workers who, for the sake of the residents, stayed at their working place throughout, were finally reunited with their families after twelve weeks of not seeing them.

It also transpired that four out of five people don't show any symptoms of the virus and are, therefore, not aware that they potentially can pass it on to people they are in contact with. So, their sacrifice was well worth the effort.

The sight of our streets is changing too. In order to avoid public transport, more and more people have taken up cycling instead and sales of bicycles have gone up by fifty-seven percent—one positive sign in an otherwise stretched economy.

9th July

Regarding COVID-19 there is still new information filtering through as we continue to learn more about this new disease.

At first, it was thought that it could be transmitted from one person to the next by tiny droplets which are produced when we cough or sneeze. But now it is said that it can also be transmitted through small particles in the air when we talk and breathe out, which makes wearing a face mask all the more essential.

We also hear that it is not yet clear how much COVID-19 has actually damaged the economy in its entirety. Some funding will be needed from the government and the chancellor has now revealed his plan for the summer.

According to him, it is vital to keep people in employment after the furlough scheme will come to an end in October, but also to create new jobs, especially for young people under twenty-five.

From giving stamp duty a holiday, to eating out from Monday to Friday at a reduced price—the scheme is not without its surprises when it comes to generosity and ingenuity, but people also wonder how the government will ever make up for the heavy borrowing which these schemes depend on.

10th July

Like so many other churches, Westminster Abbey is reopening its doors after four months of closure.

The last time it was closed for such a long time was in 1953 for the Queen's coronation. It depends for its upkeep entirely on the donations of visitors, as it does not receive any subsidy from the Church or the State.

At this time of year, it usually receives one thousand visitors every hour. But, with social distancing in place, this has been reduced to one hundred every hour and, naturally, the Abbey is feeling the pinch and is not quite sure yet how to make up for the loss.

Parish churches, too, have resumed their services but, because seats are limited as social distancing has to be observed at all times, you have to book a seat online if you want to attend.

For so long now, it had only been possible to follow a service on Zoom. Services are still kept to a minimum and the focus is on offering Sunday services. Many Christians will welcome the thought that they can visit their local church again.

11th July

The chancellor's plans to revive the economy have come under scrutiny and the question is being asked: is he really offering value for money when he tries to give people an incentive to eat out during August or to reward employers when they keep their staff on?

However, he also says that Great Britain will experience the worst recession we have ever had, maybe worse than the one in 1980. He is under no illusion, so he says, that times will be tough and that not all jobs can be kept secure.

And, as if underlining this trend, Café Rouge and Bella Italia have gone into administration, Burger King is closing some of its outlets and John Lewis is closing some of its branches, seven of them in and around London; at the same time, they will lay off one thousand three hundred of their staff. Boots, so it is said, is also reducing their staff.

But one man's loss is another man's gain. Some of them who were lucky enough to offer and produce something that has gone up in demand are thriving and doing well. Book sales have gone up, for instance, obviously because people want something to do at home when they can't go out. DIY has gone up, and supermarkets' delivery service has increased enormously.

12th July

So far, we have been told to stay at home and to stay alert, if we have to go out.

Now, with new cases of COVID-19 steadily falling, the government wants to encourage us to go out and spend some of the money we have been able to save during lockdown.

The same applies to public transport. Before, we were told: 'Avoid it if you can.' Now, this is replaced by: 'use it if you can'.

And, instead of spending too much time at home, we are told: 'Eat out to help out' and 'go out to help out'!

Relying on the British public, the government hopes that, with such an incentive, we can get the economy going again.

At the same time, more restrictions are being lifted from next Monday—beauticians, tattoo and tanning salons will open; musicians and artists are allowed to perform outdoors; gyms, leisure centres and outdoor swimming pools will follow on 25th July.

Let summer commence!

13th July

"The pandemic may have brought about much suffering and misery, but sometimes it has brought together two people again who should not have been apart from each other in the first place."

These are the words of a young man who was contacted in early May by his then-ex-girlfriend.

Just a simple 'hi' on WhatsApp, a gesture born out of boredom during lockdown.

They had drifted apart for the last eight years. Before that, in 2009, they had seen each other for one year but then the relationship became more and more complicated.

However, somehow, he had never forgotten her, despite other relationships he had had in between.

This simple WhatsApp started a conversation between them which became quite a permanent feature during the following weeks of lockdown. They even met up on one occasion, adhering to lockdown rules.

Now, they say: 'It's too soon to predict the future but it looks like we've actually got one!'

14th July

Most European countries are back in business now, and most of them are welcoming British holidaymakers.

In Italy, Greece and Spain, they are getting the seafront ready hoping that tourists will eventually arrive. As people travelling to these countries don't have to self-isolate anymore on their return, bookings with airlines are on the up.

The aviation industry obviously welcomes this move since they have been waiting for a much-needed demand in flights.

As for Scotland, Spain remains on the list where you have to quarantine and, for England, it is Portugal that escapes these air bridges as it is said that there has been a recent rise in cases.

London is hoping that at least visitors from Europe will visit this summer.

But American visitors will most likely be absent this year. They usually arrive in droves on our shores, one and a half million of them every year. But these are not normal times!

15th July

With a haircut and manicure or pedicure into the bargain, we can face the world again and look forward to a time when most things are allowed again, though not quite in the same manner as before.

'The new norm' of which everyone is talking, makes itself known wherever we go.

Nearly every shop or store has its bottle of sanitiser displayed and ready to be used when you enter. Face coverings should be worn when you use public transport or in a shop.

In Scotland, they are mandatory now whenever you are outdoors, and the Prime Minister has mentioned for the first time that this rule may also be introduced in England.

But, most of all, it's keeping your distance that is still rule number one and we should be very conscientious about this, for staying apart is still the safest way of not transmitting the virus, and, of course, washing your hands is what protects us best from catching it.

16th July

A young couple had to rearrange their wedding day twice. It was planned to take place in Cyprus in 2018. They did their bookings with Thomas Cook.

Eight months later, the company went into administration, and everything was cancelled.

They managed to reorganise it for the same date and location, but, alas, it had to be cancelled again due to the lockdown, along with a party they had organised in the UK on their return.

Now they are finally allowed to travel to Cyprus to exchange their wedding vows.

"It's been a long wait, but it was worth it," says the bride and she is now hopeful that her big day will go ahead.

However, she doesn't know yet how many guests will be able to make the trip.

Here in England, up to thirty people are now allowed to attend a wedding.

17th July

'Targeted action' is being taken every week against more than a hundred local coronavirus outbreaks, says health secretary Matt Hancock.

Factories, hospitals and other workplaces have been shut down and, in Herefordshire, a farm was put under lockdown conditions.

It's also been two weeks now since Leicester had to accept new restrictions; they are expected to be reviewed this week.

In Germany, too, a local lockdown was re-imposed when a meat processing plant was shut down, and bars, restaurants and cinemas had to close in that area. People were asked to self-isolate for fourteen days and not to travel to other districts.

Following the recent outbreak of COVID-19 in China's capital, Beijing, a lockdown has been enforced in parts of the city. People are currently prevented from leaving their neighbourhood, rail and flight services have been suspended, and schools, swimming pools and gyms are closed.

The struggle to get on top of this virus continues.

18th July

A curious story has been made public about a young man who believed that the coronavirus was nothing but a hoax.

He attended a party of COVID-19 partygoers where the message went round: "See who will catch it!" The young man in question tested positive the next day and consequently died, saying: "So it is true after all."

This is indeed a story that is hard to believe considering the fact that many have already fallen victim to the disease.

From America, we get alarming news, especially from Florida and Los Angeles where as many as sixty thousand people are affected every day. It is said that bars and restaurants were allowed to open far too soon while social distancing was hardly observed.

It is no wonder as President Trump never really accepted the gravity of the situation, treating the wearing of face masks very lightly.

Just like in this country, you come across the odd person who denies the fact that we are dealing here with a major catastrophe that, so far, has cost endless numbers of lives and still doesn't show any definite signs of abating.

19th July

More unsettling news is gradually coming to the surface.

We know now that the economy shrank by a fifth up to the month of May. However, the building and housing market is, at least tentatively, showing signs of recovery and so is the retail sector.

The indication of these early signs of an improvement is, according to scientific advice, only a 'possibility', not a 'prediction'.

As the virus lives longer in cold weather and can be transmitted more easily when we spend more time indoors, the scientists say that a second wave could turn out to be even worse than the first one. The worst-case scenario could be that more than one hundred and twenty thousand people will die from September onwards.

Therefore, the government must be prepared for all eventualities.

As a precautionary measure, face coverings will become mandatory from 24th July.

In Scotland, this is already the case, while in Wales, they only have to be worn on public transport, at least for the time being.

20th July

More than a million people have given up smoking since the pandemic hit.

This is according to the survey of 'Action on Smoking and Health.' Four in ten said that this was a direct response to the coronavirus because of the government's comment that smokers may be at risk of more severe symptoms.

Apart from that, there is also the fact that those who self-isolated might have less access to tobacco or a chance to smoke outside. Opportunities to smoke in a social environment were also few and far between.

Instead, people took up recreational activities to occupy their minds.

Many went the extra mile to find new avenues and outlets and started new skills as well as new sources of occupational therapies which could provide them with a new sense of having actually achieved something.

More women took up baking, sewing and other handicrafts, and many men focused on technical achievements and DIY jobs. There seems to be an endless variety of things to do or to make.

21st July

More reassuring and encouraging words from the Prime Minister: looking ahead, he is hoping that, by November, restrictions will be far less likely and relaxed to such an extent that a return to a normal life can be expected and we can look forward to Christmas.

He is giving employers the chance to use their discretion when it comes to going back to work. For some, this will mean continuing to work from home, whereas others will return to their working place.

Local authorities are given special powers to act quickly if and when they have to deal with a flare-up of infection locally.

He promised to give the NHS another three billion pounds.

In case of another outbreak of the disease, the Nightingale Hospitals are protected, and the use of private hospitals is funded.

But, on a more optimistic note, it is likely that we can expect a return to normality which will also mean that there is more contact with family and friends, something that will become especially important when we approach the Christmas season.

22nd July

SARS-CoV-2 is the name of the virus currently in circulation. It is no longer the same virus that started in Wuhan in China. It is mutating.

The question is, however, whether it is more lethal and infectious and whether it could be a threat to the progress which is being made to find a vaccine.

The Prime Minister wants to avoid a second national lockdown for obvious reasons but, in Scotland, the latest developments show that there is presently the highest number of cases since 21st June.

As to the number of cases around the globe, there are now two hundred and sixty thousand people who are affected. The highest number of cases are in the US, Brazil, India and South Africa. It is the first time that the number of cases has exceeded a quarter of a million.

In England, however, the first music event took place in Manchester in front of a wide audience.

People tried to keep their distance but, as the night went on, social distancing got blurred eventually. People wanted to savour every minute of the event after the long absence of four months.

23rd July

A first attendance in church. It was good to touch base again with one's Christian roots. It puts things in a better and sounder perspective.

The world is so full of news about COVID-19 and has been for such a long time by now, that it is good to shut the door on it for a while and enter, instead, a world that is still wholesome, unchanged and more profound.

The present situation has brought about so many changes, so many upheavals for so many, that we need an anchor and some guidelines—not only those given by the government but guidelines which also assist us when dealing inwardly with all the uprooting events.

The ship which was shaken by the big waves of the open sea enters the harbour in order to find rest and peace. We step on solid ground again and give thanks for having withstood the perils while the storm was raging.

And, with a deep sigh of relief, we say: it is good to be alive!

24th July

Nurse Ayesha Orlanda who is fifty-two years old has been given an emotional send-off from the hospital.

She is a senior sister at Bradford Royal Infirmary and became critically ill with the coronavirus.

Eventually, she had to be put on a ventilator. She fought for her life for more than nine and a half weeks and finally recovered.

"I am one of the lucky ones," was her comment when she was finally sufficiently recovered to leave the hospital.

She strongly felt that she had been given "a second chance in life".

She greatly appreciated the constant care she received during her illness.

And the staff from four wards gathered to applaud her as she left. She had been in intensive care for forty-one days after being admitted in May.

Now she is looking forward to returning to her family.

25th July

Tea, coffee, biscuits and a good book—that's what most of us wanted during lockdown.

This is the revelation of the market research firm Kantar. According to their report, people splashed out an additional £24 million on tea and coffee and an extra £19 million on biscuits in the past three months.

Reading was also up on the list, according to the publisher Bloomsbury—book sales were up by almost a fifth compared to last year. Bestsellers included the J.K. Rowling's Harry Potter series and books related to the Black Lives Matter campaign, which sprung into life ever since George Floyd was so needlessly killed by the rude hands of an American policeman.

It had long repercussions both in America, New Zealand and England, with demonstrations taking place just about anywhere, despite the virus and social distancing regulations.

In Bristol and London, statues that had anything to do with the slave trade in past centuries were deliberately pulled down.

This new movement, which was started as a direct result of the killing, will stay with us and will make itself known in many areas of public life where racism can still be found to be the root of the problem.

26th July

Lottie spent the first month of the lockdown in her bedroom because her sitting room reminded her too much of the abuse she had endured.

Hers is only one voice of the many victims who suffered abuse at the hands of their partners.

The Novec Switch project is a charity organisation that offers housing and therapy for so many who, without it, could not have escaped mistreatment during lockdown.

With the help of such organisations, women find hope and self-worth again and it gives them the encouragement they need in order to survive and look forward to a new chapter in their lives.

Receiving attention and finding a listening ear is often the first step to dealing with, not only the physical pain, but also the mental scars which are inflicted by sometimes horrendous circumstances.

Quite often this kind of intervention leads to a positive change in their troubled lives.

27th July

You cannot but notice the clear signs of a changed world wherever you go in London.

The doors of small fringe theatres seem to be shut forever. Some pubs look abandoned and not open to the public any longer, and shops indicate exactly where you are supposed to enter and where to exit.

Small businesses and stores in those side streets which are located away from the main road and traffic, are barricaded up and closed for good.

Wherever there might be a queue for entering a store or a bank, there are signposts on the pavement telling you where you should stand which avoids being too close to the person who is in front of you.

Despite the financial support that the government is trying to provide, it cannot be ignored that the virus has taken its toll on what was once the vibrant city of London.

This virus which exceeds any other virus we might have confronted and dealt with in the past has thrown the entire world into turmoil to such a degree as it has never happened before.

And, still, we must confess that we don't know enough about it yet in order to be able to combat it successfully.

28th July

People are now obliged to wear a face covering whenever they enter a shop when they want to purchase something to wear or fetch something to eat.

But, for the first time we get some comments from the community of the seventy thousand deaf people in the UK.

As they depend on the UK sign language but also on lip reading, wearing a mask over the mouth and nose can turn out to be a real handicap for them, as you cannot see the mouth of the speaker.

What is, therefore, required is a face mask where the area around the mouth is covered in a transparent piece of plastic.

"I have the feeling that I am missing out on a lot of information," says Mark who is deaf, "and that makes me feel even more isolated and alone."

"It has a direct impact on my mental health. I lack communication and this is bad news for our community as deaf people. I don't think this problem is sufficiently realised by the society at large."

A comment which is well worth being listened to and considered.

29th July

Luton is experiencing a new spike of the virus with sixteen new cases in one street alone. All public places, including gyms, playgrounds and cinemas, have been closed.

It is also reported that Spain is having a second wave which means that new restrictions have been put in place. Travellers returning from there have now to go into quarantine for fourteen days.

For the first time, the Prime Minister has spoken up and said that the virus which we know so little about, has to be studied very carefully and lessons have to be learned.

When we first tried to deal with the rapidly growing infection rate, its tremendous impact on life, in general, was largely underestimated.

The most critical point is whether all of us are willing to give up immediate gratification of something we want to have or do, of our plans and intentions, and learn to make do with less, making always sure that safety takes precedence.

30th July

Stephen, who is a pilot, caught the virus on one of his flights and had to be admitted to hospital in Vietnam. There, he was fighting for his life. For one hundred and fourteen days he was on a ventilator. His lungs were badly affected, and he lost the use of his legs.

When he was eventually over the worst, a long period of rehabilitation began, and he took his first steps with the help of crutches.

He is now looking forward to being able to fly again but is still undergoing a lengthy recovery process.

When asked what advice he could give to people, he said:

"The virus has to be taken extremely seriously and people do well to observe all the guidelines that are given. Don't complain about social distancing because it might save your life. This virus can hit you at any moment if you don't take care, no matter how old or how young you are."

31ˢᵗ July

Six-year-old Faith was out looking for a magazine she could read during lockdown but there was pretty little she found appealing and worth buying.

So, she and her mum, Serina, sat down and designed one themselves.

It would turn out to be the first magazine for young black girls and they are overjoyed because the magazine has already sold eleven thousand copies.

It shows again how necessity and unusual circumstances can bring out the creative ingenuity in us, provided we allow it to override the negative aspect that the situation has in tow and turn this into a positive.

Those not strong enough or willing to try something new will experience frustration or boredom which can turn into the desire to make up for lost time when it is all over.

But the opposite is true for those who use their misfortune to their own advantage.

1ˢᵗ August

Simon was sleeping rough in the doorways of Manchester. When the lockdown hit in March, he was moved to a room with a bathroom in the Holiday Inn.

Simon had lost his partner four years ago.

He had shared her flat. When she died, he lost the use of the flat and became homeless.

As he said, he was not used to sleeping on cardboard boxes and not being able to feed himself properly.

So, when he was given this comfortable accommodation in the Holiday Inn, his life changed dramatically.

On arrival, he was very thin and dirty. He put on weight and was generally looked after.

This experience made him determined not to return to his old life but to try everything to maintain a decent life.

He will, however, need help and support.

2nd August

The coronavirus stubbornly resists defeat and keeps on raising its head in different parts of the country and abroad.

The Prime Minister announced that tighter restrictions are being imposed in the North of England, particularly in Greater Manchester, East Lancashire and West Yorkshire, which will affect some four million people.

Any further easing of restrictions which were planned for the beginning of August is being postponed for another fortnight, which means that bowling alleys, skating rings and sporting events continue to be unavailable.

From the rest of Europe, we hear of similar outbreaks, especially in Luxembourg and Belgium.

Eastern countries like Romania, Serbia and Croatia show similar spikes, and countries are considering closing their borders again.

On a more hopeful note, The Prime Minister also mentioned that, on the whole, the number of cases continues to fall in England, but he warns that, with the number of cases rising in the rest of Europe, we must be prepared for a second wave.

3rd August

With all the reports coming through about a marked increase in domestic abuse and mental aggravation, it is indeed a relief when people are telling their stories where the lockdown and working from home has added to their mental well-being.

It is providing them with more quality time spent on their own or with the family, and it is also said that it helped them to save money on fares which could then be put away for a future holiday, when travelling will be a bit more normal again.

It seems to be true that all the complaints, the moaning and groaning, and some of the strong criticisms reflect a certain attitude which, in a state of negation, tends to pull everything down and then it is all seen in a thoroughly negative light.

At a time when we are forced to question and reconsider our values, our priorities and habits, only a certain percentage of us seems to be able to have the gift of, not only adjusting to the changed conditions, but also appreciating some of the things which these conditions can provide, and this is important when we are exposed and challenged in our humanity in so many ways.

4th August

While English restaurants, cafés and pubs are getting ready to take bookings for the next four weeks when the Eat Out-Help Out scheme comes into action and people can have a meal out for only half the cost, Australia is entering a serious second wave of the virus.

There is a complete shutdown of all public places, and even a curfew is being declared at night, all in aid of the attempt to get on top of this new outbreak which is more widely spread out than the first one was.

Australia was one of the countries which recovered very quickly from the initial spread of the disease but is now struggling to cope with the second wave.

Here, on home ground, the scientists are able to give us some more hopeful news as they have now found a way to test whether you have the virus or other infections, and to have the result in as little as ninety minutes. This is not only good news for the winter months but could greatly help in the effort to avoid any further outbreaks on a national scale.

5th August

Figures from HM Revenue & Customs show that the government has covered the wages of more than nine million employers under its job retention scheme, with the Treasury paying out almost £34 billion since April.

A further £78 billion has gone to meet income support claims for self-employed workers.

What will happen when these schemes come to an end in October?

Pizza Express is the latest restaurant group to undertake a financial restructuring after trading was halted by the pandemic. The company is considering closing sixty-seven sites which would mean a loss of one thousand one hundred jobs.

Meanwhile, Curry PC World is making eight hundred workers redundant, as the chain is overhauling its store management structure in order to adapt to an increase in online sales.

6ᵗʰ August

It is all about local intervention which seems to be the way forward in order to avoid any further major lockdowns.

This time it is Aberdeen where four cases have become fifty-four and, so, all restaurants, pubs and bars have been asked to close, with the exception of schools.

Schools will be the last ones to close in order to safeguard against any further shortfall in education.

In Scotland, schools will reopen in the second half of August, whereas, in England, it will be in September that all the schools are meant to open their doors again.

For the first time, grades in Scotland were given by the teachers and their estimation of the students as no exams had taken place.

Now, during the holiday season, some parents are planning a 'staycation', while others want to go further afield, across to Europe but, let it be said: the reproduction rate of the virus is dangerously on the up.

7th August

According to recent research, it has become apparent that the slump in the economy is not as bad as had been predicted.

It was assumed that, because of the pandemic, it would shrink by fourteen percent; but the latest calculations show that it only shrank by nine percent.

It is expected, however, that it will take longer to recover, and that full recovery will only come by the end of 2021 provided there won't be a second wave.

The government is trying its best to boost the economy, but it will take time while this pandemic is still going on.

From the high street, we hear of more job losses.

W.H. Smith is closing its outlets in railway stations and airports which will amount to one thousand one hundred losses among their workforces.

William Hill is also reducing the number of its stores, but employees will be absorbed by the remaining ones.

9th August

So far, the start of the coronavirus in this country, its rise and fall, has provided enough material to fill the pages; but now, when the immediate danger of it has somewhat subsided, any news about it has naturally decreased.

The lockdown, which was then introduced, had given rise to many thoughts, speculations, fears and expectations.

Now that the virus is being kept under control by the imposition of localised restrictions, the hope is that, in this way, the country as a whole can look forward to more freedom.

The latest hotspot where restrictions had to be put in place is Preston in the North of England while, here in the South, life has taken on an almost normal rhythm again and, rather than talking about the illness, it is the impact it has on the economy which is in the forefront of people's thinking.

10th August

There is a lot of controversy going on about the question of whether or not all children should be sent back to school in September.

At the centre of the debate is naturally their safety. With the coronavirus almost everywhere in retreat, it stands to reason that the Prime Minister calls it his 'moral duty' that all pupils should be back in education in September.

Schools have been busy to ensure all necessary precautions are in place which include keeping social distancing at all times and minimising contact with other pupils during break time.

However, there is still a lot of resistance among parents, and even among MPs, as there are those who maintain that September is too soon.

The Prime Minister, however, insists that it is safe for schools to welcome everybody back and, as the Prime Minister has access to all the latest scientific developments, he should perhaps be listened to.

12th August

Just as airlines have been hit badly by the pandemic, so has the demand for cruise holidays.

As a result, the English Channel has become home to a number of cruise liners that have nowhere to go. They are moored out at sea because it is either too costly or there is not enough room for them to be parked in the port.

They have received a great deal of interest as they have become a new part of Britain's coastal scene and have turned into a tourist attraction in their own right—with one entrepreneur offering boat trips in order to get closer to the massive ships.

On the other hand, this underlines the many problems the pandemic has created and continues to create as far as the economy is concerned.

It is said that, for the first time in eleven years, the economy has gone into recession.

A report published by the Office of National Statistics said that, though the economy bounced back in June when the lockdown was lifted, GDP was only a sixth of the level recorded in February.

14th August

France has been added to the list of those countries where you have to go into quarantine on your return to the UK.

It will come into force at four a.m. tomorrow and people tried to cut their holiday short in order to get a return ticket and go home before the deadline.

There are, at present, half a million Brits on holiday in France and both ferries and the Eurotunnel are fully booked.

People coming from as far as the South of France took their chance but were asked to stay away as they only added to the chaos.

Here, in England, some more restrictions have been eased during the weekend.

From tomorrow, casinos, ice rings and bowling alleys are all allowed to open their doors to help the economy, and, for the children, the indoor playgrounds will be open for their entertainment.

19ᵗʰ August

Right now, the attention has turned to those who have to pay rent for their accommodation.

The ban on evictions was introduced in March to protect renters during the pandemic but it is coming to an end next Sunday.

It is estimated that about a quarter of a million people have fallen into arrears in recent months and could lose their homes, especially when the furlough scheme will also end later this year.

Wales has already extended its protection scheme and Scotland has proposed doing so.

More bad news is coming from well-known brands in the high street like Marks & Spencer, for instance. Redundancies seem unavoidable.

A-level students in England, we hear, are most disappointed because their results were significantly downgraded after no exams had taken place. Now the government has taken a U-turn and accepted that the assessment of their teachers should determine the performance of the students.

20th August

Among all the negative aspects which COVID-19 inflicted on the nation, there is one mundane feature where it contributes to a certain trend in the world of fashion.

Along with the introduction of face coverings comes the fact that we can no longer openly display our faces. It also means that there is less demand for any kind of foundation or make-up.

But a study has shown that, since lockdown began, the sale of various eye make-up products has gone up, for it is, after all, the eyes that are noticed most in an otherwise covered-up face. The same study suggests that the sale of lipstick has come down.

As to the face coverings themselves, they, too, have become a fashion item.

Their variety of materials is astonishing—from the plain blue and white versions to the highly sophisticated colourful patterned kind, the choice is endless, and they are on sale in most stores now along with other fashionable items.

21st August

France has reported more than four thousand cases of COVID-19 for the first time since May, with officials saying that the virus is now circulating in major cities and, this time, more among younger people.

But, despite the increasing number of cases, the French education minister has ruled out postponing the start of the new school year in September.

Cases are also increasing in Spain, Germany and Italy.

Portugal, however, has been taken off the list of those countries where you have to quarantine on your return, whereas Croatia, Austria, Trinidad and Tobago have been added to this list.

Typically, people who, for many reasons prefer a 'staycation' rather than going to a foreign country, welcome greatly the reopening of the Science and Victoria & Albert Museums, and the village of Harry Potter is also welcoming visitors again.

22ⁿᵈ August

The whole world is waiting for a COVID-19 vaccine. There are by now at least thirty experimental vaccines, and trials on humans are underway. Thousands of volunteers have thus been immunised.

In fact, in England, would-be volunteers are campaigning to be allowed to participate in so-called 'challenge trials' whereby the attempt is made to speed up the development of a suitable vaccine.

The trials would involve receiving the vaccine which is then followed by a dose of live coronavirus a few weeks later in order to check whether the vaccine has protected them.

Alastair Fraser-Urquart, eighteen, is such a volunteer. He has just received his A-level results. "I am in the lowest risk category for COVID-19; so why won't I make the choice and help save other people who would have to deal with it far worse than me," he says.

So, what does Alistair's family think? "They are not really opposed to the idea," is the answer.

25th August

The last weekend in August is approaching with its bank holiday when, normally, the Notting Hill Carnival gets into full swing. It's a longstanding tradition and costumes are extravagant.

Usually, two million people gather in the streets of Notting Hill and Portobello Road and watch the exotic parades, taste the culinary treats and listen to the typically rhythmic sounds of the Caribbean drums.

But, this year, the festival can only be watched online as any street party of more than thirty people is strictly forbidden and will be punished with a hefty fine.

Similarly, the Last Night of the Proms is also due to take place online only, of course, while the seats in the Royal Albert Hall remain empty.

Another yearly fundraising event, the London Marathon, provides an income for many charities and, in its absence, participants had to reinvent themselves by offering certain sporty activities online which, so far, have proved to be a real success.

26th August

This is the time when school children have either already returned to school, like in Scotland, or will do so in a week's time. In the school buildings, there is now a one-way system and sanitisers at every corner.

Tables and chairs have been shifted in accordance with guidelines for social distancing.

In Scotland, it is already mandatory for pupils to wear a face mask in communal areas but, in England, it is left to the discretion of the Head which was a welcomed concession for most of them.

A study has shown that, during lockdown, there was a lower level of anxiety among young people because they did not have to worry about school-related issues.

But now pupils are quite willing and ready to return to the classroom and to see their friends again.

28th August

Social distancing rules presented many problems when it came to filming for television. A crew of the BBC soap Eastenders found an imaginative way to create intimate scenes by using the actors' real-life partners. They have been drafted in to allow moments of intimacy to be played out when the soap will resume.

This move was just one of several measures which had to be taken in order to keep cast and crew safe on set.

In order to follow social distancing guidelines on indoor sets, like in the Queen Victoria pub, producers had to think laterally. So clear Perspex screens, which are invisible to the camera, are being placed between the actors who share the scene.

This allows the producers to bring people really close together which provides a large degree of intimacy to the performance that would otherwise not be there.

The programme, which had to stop because of COVID-19, will resume 7th September, with all necessary measures in place, including a one-way system around the studios and temperature checking for the cast and crew.

29th August

It's the August Bank Holiday with a difference. They are none of the usual events held at the end of August.

However, it is estimated that eighteen million journeys will be made by car alone.

This is partly due to the fact that people are taking breaks in the UK this summer, and many will be returning home if they have been on a holiday abroad.

Some will have been on short trips to make the most of a long weekend.

Would-be travellers, who have had their plans thwarted, are being offered ways to get their flying fix without going abroad.

Companies have devised a number of ways to give customers an experience of plane travelling, from selling pairs of pyjamas to the sale of airline meals complete with tray, and there are even flights to choose from which go nowhere: it means taking off and landing at the same airport.

30th August

A young thirteen-year-old discovered his love for music when he lost his mother two years ago, and he decided, there and then, to become really good at it.

So, he used his time in Lockdown to practice the piano a lot and he composed a piece of music dedicated to his mother.

As for the many school children who are due to return to school any time now, they are looking forward to a fresh experience, but the government still has a hard time convincing nervous parents that it is safe to do so.

The danger of catching COVID-19 is minimal among young ones and, if they do, it is never very serious. The few who died from it have had underlying health problems.

A debate is also going on about students returning to universities. Their leaders say, again, that measures have been taken to make it safe for students to have their lectures partly on a one-to-one basis and partly online.

Millions of students are returning, and the pessimists say that they will trigger off a second wave.

4th September

Quarantine periods are decided upon and lifted again, only to be decided upon again at a later date, and these rules differ whether we are in Scotland, Wales or England and Northern Ireland.

Holidaymakers who opted for a holiday in Greece, Portugal or Spain are naturally annoyed by these sudden changes, while the government insists that only swift action can prevent us from importing the virus as it can be found in these countries.

The time seems forgotten when most of us pulled together and felt united by the necessity of overcoming the power this deadly virus has on us.

With the relaxation of some of the restrictions, our personal interests and desires were rekindled and stirred us into complaining about further bothersome limitations of our freedom which, this time, are, as many of us think, totally unnecessary.

But this can only have one result: in many countries, the number of cases is on the rise again. Will we ever learn?

8th September

The UK might have reached what can be called a tipping point. There are six thousand new cases in the last two days and government officials expressed their concern.

It is true that most of these cases affect predominantly a younger age group whose life is mostly not at risk when they catch the virus, and that means that the death rate has remained at the lower end.

But, unless the younger population alters their pattern of behaviour, the danger is that the virus might spread to the older population and the more vulnerable, too.

It cannot be stressed often enough that this virus cannot be taken lightly. There are even reports coming through where younger people suffer from what is called, 'long COVID'.

Weeks later, after having contracted the illness, people have still symptoms of bad health, like shortness of breath, weakness of limbs and fatigue. Some of them need a whole programme of rehabilitation after leaving hospital.

As one young woman expressed it after testing positive in June: "I just want my life back. I still feel sick and unable to go back to work."

9th September

As from next Monday a ban on gatherings with more than six people will be introduced in England.

The fact that it will become law will make it easier for the police to issue a fine of £100 to those who are ignoring the new law. This ban was apparently necessary because of the sharp increase in cases of COVID-19.

The number of cases is four times higher than it was in mid-July and can no longer be ignored.

Wales, Scotland and Northern Ireland will make their own decisions.

Another matter of concern is the vast number of furloughed employees when the scheme will end next month. Many fear that they will be made redundant and will then rely on the state for support.

The world of the theatre and its artists is equally in distress. They claim that, unless they are allowed to open again soon, the damage will be long-lived and irreversible which will have a permanent effect on our city's cultural centres.

11th September

The R-number, by which we measure the spread of the disease, has risen above one. It is currently 1.2 in England which means that it has reached a level that is dangerously high. That level should always be below one as it was during June and July when it was 0.7.

But, since the end of August, there has been a marked resurgence of the virus, especially in the North of England as well as in Birmingham.

New restrictions had to be reintroduced. Surprisingly, the age group which is mostly affected this time is the eighteen to twenty-four-year-olds. The trace and testing facilities have proved to be very effective.

The new law of meeting with no more than six people has now also been introduced in Wales and Scotland, and we hear the voices of some who find this an utter nuisance.

But, after all, what is more important? Should not number one on our list of considerations be the defeat of the virus?

So, why not do what we can to combat the danger that this virus certainly entails, and stay safe?

To a large extent, it is really up to us. It is our sense of responsibility that is in question here.

14th September

One theatre in the West End has taken the plunge by putting on a new musical called "Six".

After all the dire news concerning the theatre and its producers and performers, after months of closure during the lockdown which meant losing money in a big way, and after a revival was indeed put into question, it is encouraging to hear that at least one theatre dared to open its doors to the public again.

It was and still is a risk that they took, but people are already queuing since early morning. People seem to be ready to support the industry.

The general mood at the moment can be described as being conducive to the existing circumstances.

People seem willing to follow the guidelines as well as they can in view of the fact that the Christmas season will, hopefully, bring a relaxation of the rules, which then will benefit the hospitality sector, the high street and the revival of the family Christmas as we know it.

18th September

The surge of cases continues. There have been sixty thousand new cases between 4th and 14th September—six thousand cases per day.

The testing system is presently under a lot of strain because of an increase in demand, and people have to travel hundreds of miles to get tested.

The matter is being looked into, and care homes are again mentioned in the context of insufficient testing facilities.

The North of England and the Midlands are subject to stricter restrictions, and England is considering closing the hospitality sector for several weeks in view of the fact that such a step may avoid another national lockdown.

However, the scientists warn that, without further intervention, we might have a second major outbreak by the end of October and the death rate, which is still low at the moment, might start to rise again.

They stressed, above all, that everyone *must* keep to the guidelines.

23rd September

At this crucial point when the course of the epidemic could turn either way—when it could either rise again to a level where it continues to cause major destruction or can be curbed by new restrictions—the Prime Minister addressed the nation in a ministerial broadcast.

He reminded us how the national lockdown had brought us together and he pointed out that we can defeat this virus provided we have the discipline to do what must be done.

He then announced the new restrictions: pubs and restaurants will close at ten p.m., and it will be table service only.

As for weddings, the number of guests is being reduced from thirty to fifteen only. Any gathering must not exceed six people, and those who do not adhere to these guidelines can be charged a fine of £200 if it's the first time.

It goes without saying that sports events will be played indoors and can only be followed virtually.

The question which is on everyone's mind is: what will the future hold for us?

25th September

Young people are particularly badly affected, be it in their work or their private life. Many of them have lost their job and have to find alternative ways of earning money.

There is the actress who abandoned her acting career and fell back on the skills she has to help people with their make-up.

Instead of going to the office, a young woman decided to make jewellery and sell it online. Another turned her attention to baking and hopes that her business will take off.

And then there are the young couples who wanted to get married. One such couple had planned a big wedding with one hundred and twenty guests early this May. Then they had to rethink in order to follow the rule of having thirty guests only. Now they are down to fifteen invitations.

As we heard, it all went well, social distancing was in place, no music or mingling among guests, and it turned out to be a great day after all.

This is the time to get inventive and to be flexible if we don't want our life to come to a complete standstill.

29th September

The death rate worldwide has now exceeded one million, and more than half of these deaths occurred in America, Brazil and India.

In view of this sobering thought, it is hard to understand why people rebel against the closing time of ten p.m. as far as restaurants, bars and pubs are concerned.

We hear that people group together after closing time to find some outlets where they can buy more booze, obviously quite oblivious to the spread of a very contagious disease.

And, yet, the figures show that the number of cases is rising on a daily basis, the average being four thousand a day.

Surely, people can recognise that the measures that have been taken by the government are not to punish us, but, on the contrary, to save as many lives as possible.

Are we responsible adults or disobedient children who must gratify their every whim? Fortunately, such a minority of wrongdoers is not denying the fact that most of us accept the consequences that this pandemic has created on home ground and the world stage.

30th September

There is no doubt that this pandemic is the most severe and most testing time our planet has ever experienced in peaceful times, and there is still no end in sight.

The Christmas season is not so far off now, and already we know that the attractions of Winter Wonderland in Hyde Park will not be open this year.

Christmas markets will be closed and, as for the theatregoers, there will be no pantomimes to cheer us during the festive season.

Artists know how important the pantos are; they are an essential aspect financially. They mostly bring in the money that will see them through the rest of the year.

A group of actors and actresses, dressed in their panto costumes, walked up to Downing Street to make themselves heard and asked for better support.

They are just one section of our society whose very existence is endangered because of the situation we are facing right now.

And, meanwhile, there is no respite: cases are going up and so is the death rate now.

2nd October

The London Marathon will take place on Sunday. But it will be a virtual marathon. Far and wide, runners will perform in towns and villages and, whoever reaches the finishing line, will receive a medal.

The elite runners, however, will stay overnight in a secret hotel. They have been tested for security reasons and they even practice in the garden of the hotel. They will run in St. James's Park in Central London.

The comment about the event is: 'Will it be the same?'—Certainly not! 'Will it be conducted in the same spirit?'—Definitely! It takes more than the spread of a virus to break such a longstanding tradition!

It takes some stamina indeed not to be discouraged or overwhelmed by existing conditions and it demands a lot of perseverance and undiminished enthusiasm to complete the run without the cheering crowds!

5th October

Ninety-two-year-old grandmother, Rita, was "kidnapped" by her granddaughter, Anne, and taken home in an ambulance.

She had been put in a reputable care home before the time the coronavirus struck and had received frequent visits from her family.

Then the lockdown put a stop to these visits and, even at the time when restrictions were eased, Anne could only visit her grandmother twice a month and they had to keep well apart from each other.

The doctor said that she was approaching the end of her life. She had lost a lot of weight and become very frail.

Her son, Anne's father, was unhappy about the situation. His mother had helped to raise the children when their mother had to go to work.

So, Anne took the initiative and brought Rita back to her family.

"It was a proper heist," she commented and added: "Now Grandma is with us, and she is receiving proper care, as my mother was a nurse."

6th October

On a previous occasion, when things were still on the up, the Prime Minister had urged people to visit cinemas again. But now we get the news that Cineworld is temporarily closing its UK and US venues which will affect forty-five thousand jobs. He had said that he "would encourage people to go out and enjoy the cinema and support 'movie theatres'".

But his encouragement was not enough to stop the Odeon chain from announcing that it was reducing the opening hours to weekends only in its one hundred and twenty cinemas.

The executive of the Vue cinema chain said that there was "a pent-up demand like never before, but our problem right now is that we have no movies."

A further delay to the release of the latest James Bond film—announced last Friday—was "a big blow," he said. The film is called: 'No Time to Die', and Daniel Craig plays the role of James Bond.

Delays and cancellations are only too common in this industry, even during a time such as it is at present when it really matters.

8th October

President Trump and the first lady were both ill with the virus; but the President, who is seventy-four, was given an experimental drug in hospital and he seems to have recovered within a few days.

Now he wants all Americans to have this drug available and, so he said, he will offer it for free.

Meanwhile, here in Europe, there still is a constant rise in cases just about everywhere. In Italy, it is now mandatory to wear a face mask wherever you are. In Belgium, pubs and restaurants have been closed again.

Paris has taken the same measures. Germany has the highest number of cases since April and, in Eastern Europe, cases are quickly mounting.

Scotland has closed pubs and restaurants while, here in England, they have to shut at ten p.m., but further measures are expected.

The early closing hours have caused a lot of friction between the government and the hospitality sector and even some ministers are against it. There will now be a vote about it.

12th October

The constant rise in cases has reached a crucial point where the Nightingale Hospitals are back in action to minimise the effect this has on the NHS.

In order to avoid a second national lockdown, which would have catastrophic consequences for the economy as a whole, the government is now announcing that a three-tier system will be put in place in order to deal with local outbreaks.

The three tiers are: medium, high and very high. 'Medium' means that the rule of six and closing time at ten will apply. 'High' will see further restrictions, and 'very high' implies that there will be no household mixing in the home, and pubs, cafés, and casinos will be closed.

The chancellor has come up with a new support system when the furlough scheme will come to an end by the end of October.

16th October

The merciless battle continues here as everywhere in the rest of Europe. The daily news we are getting tells us that cases are rising more rapidly than expected.

Nearly half the country has been moved to tier two, that is, high alert. It means that different households are not allowed to mix indoors and the rule of six applies to meetings outdoors.

Pubs and restaurants remain open but must close at ten p.m.

London, too, will be under these new restrictions as of tonight and those who try to ignore the imposed rules may have to face a fine of £10,000 and, sadly, people do try not to abide by new regulations.

In West London, the police broke up a wedding party where more than a hundred guests were present when only fifteen are allowed.

Street parties were going on the night before these restrictions came into force but, fortunately, the majority concludes: 'We don't know what the future holds, but let's do what we can to control the virus!'

20th October

The number of deaths rose by one-third in only seven days and cases keep on mounting.

In Belgium, they go so far as saying that the authorities have totally lost control of the situation.

Closer to home, Liverpool and Lancashire are the only places where tier three has been imposed.

The government is at loggerheads with Greater Manchester which, according to the plan assigned to that area, should be on the 'very high' alert level, but the mayor of Manchester refuses to cooperate, claiming that the £22 million offered by the government is not enough for businesses to survive.

Somehow, one gets the impression that the plan which they have worked out by incorporating the three-tier system is very logical if one wants to avoid another national lockdown, but people are tired of any restrictions by now.

The Prime Minister has not the backing of the opposition party and there are, as always, many who much rather complain than cooperate.

23rd October

Millions of people are going to live under stricter guidelines as of tonight.

In Wales, they will start to impose what they call a 'firebreak' lockdown which will last until 9th November. Children, who will be on half term next week, get another week away from school. Bars and restaurants and all non-essential shops will be closed.

Scotland will introduce a five-tier system which will come into effect in a week's time. In England, Greater Manchester, South Yorkshire and Nottingham will be in tier three from tonight.

Schools will remain open, but bars, restaurants, casinos and gyms will be closed. Northern Ireland is already living under tighter restrictions.

The chancellor has announced that a new system of support for all those hardest hit by the pandemic will come into action in order to help, especially, the hospitality sector, but many say that it is too little too late. The future will tell.

24th October

There are videos available on the news where people who have recovered from COVID-19 describe their experiences.

One woman could hardly remember having been moved to intensive care and, when she woke up, she thought it was the following day. But, in fact, it was forty-five days later.

When one listens to these videos, it becomes patently clear that they are all unanimous in saying that it is a horrific illness that indeed can kill you, and they all warn about being negligent or complacent about it.

They all recommend that you do your bit for the country; wear your mask, follow the guidelines and, yes, listen to the government.

One man, who is now back home again, is still struggling to get his life back. Every step he takes is still an effort, and that is many weeks after leaving hospital.

All of them praise the care they received from the NHS.

25th October

Apart from these voices who speak about battling with COVID-19 and the devastation it had on their health and general well-being, there are those voices who claim to have analysed the facts logically and in a so-called detached way.

They speak of this second wave as a "hysteria pandemic" which mainly exists in the minds of people and has little to do with reality.

But it cannot be denied that people are still being treated in intensive care and are dying from it—whether the number is four hundred or forty a week is not the issue here—and that this illness is still a force to be reckoned with.

Those who have lost loved ones in this way will certainly agree that the danger is real, and it is, therefore, the responsibility of each country to take the necessary steps to minimise the damage, and to do so to the best of their ability.

This is not an easy task when one considers how many different opinions exist among us, and each claim to have the right answer and a better idea of how things should be handled.

24th October

There is a lot of mention in the news lately that, during lockdown or even during the time of tighter restrictions, people are not only affected physically but also mentally.

News about depression, alcoholism and any kind of abuse can be heard more frequently.

The increase is quite alarming.

However, that is only half the story. Those people who have a strong negative reaction to spending more time at home are very likely to have already had issues before the lockdown started.

The other side of the coin is the many who see a new opportunity in these new circumstances and adapt accordingly. For them, it's the time to try something different or to take up something which they are interested in but hadn't the time to pursue it.

Some find their vocation in reaching out and helping others who need support, either by a frequent phone call or in person, and so make their contribution by being useful.

It depends on our attitude, that state of mind which allows us to make the best of every day. It demands courage and a certain amount of healthy discipline.

28th October

They advertise now "Halloween at home". There won't be any trick or treating and no Guy Fawkes Night party. The only thing that matters is staying safe.

Students are beginning to wonder whether they will be able to go home for Christmas, and attendance in schools has seen a marked reduction.

In some European countries, the death rate has gone up by forty percent last week, especially in countries like Italy, Spain and also Russia, which have now made the wearing of face masks mandatory.

People have grown weary of restrictions and news about the virus. Everybody is longing for a good slice of normal life but, instead, find themselves avoiding contact with other people, including loved ones and friends.

Others wonder whether they will still have a job to go back to when all this is over, but will it ever be over, one begins to wonder.

The toy manufacturers, however, are hoping for an increase in sales. The lockdown has already been the trigger for a greater demand and, with Christmas approaching, this could well continue to be a prosperous year.

5th November

And, so, the day has finally arrived: since midnight, England is under lockdown for the second time. It is meant to last for four weeks, until the 2nd of December, in the hope that families can still get together for Christmas.

Schools, colleges and universities are allowed to remain open, but all non-essential shops have to close.

The furlough scheme has been extended until the end of March. However, there are more big companies that close down branches and declare redundancies.

On a brighter note: the father of a six-year-old daughter made news when, during the last lockdown, he built a shopping street Harry Potter style inside a cupboard, in order to hide it from her while he was working on it.

He reconstructed the scenes down to the smallest detail. As it was going to be a surprise, he mainly had to work at night when his daughter was asleep.

It turned out to be a wonderful surprise for this very special girl.

6th November

Remembrance Day will be celebrated differently this year. There won't be any people lining the streets and there won't be any open displays of remembering the dead.

Instead, people are asked to be on their doorsteps for a salute on Sunday evening.

With the lockdown having begun, there are very few people in the streets. Many have gracefully accepted this second lockdown, whereas others revolt and hang out to demonstrate.

But news from Wales is giving us a stark warning: in one family, the mother (seventy-four) and her two sons (forty-two and forty-four) died within five days of each other and Claire, the widow, is heartbroken and tells us that the father keeps on saying: "It should have been me!"

Such stories remind us all that we must accept the inevitable and bear it with patience whatever this virus throws at us.

No one is exempt and we should, therefore, feel a sense of solidarity when dealing with such an unpredictable and forceful enemy.

10ᵗʰ November

There is some encouraging news regarding a possible vaccine.

Pfizer has designed a vaccine that will provide protection of ninety percent against the virus. There will have to be two separate inoculations with three weeks in between.

The UK has already stocked enough of this vaccine to vaccinate twenty million people and, according to the Health Secretary Matt Hancock, it is likely that the vaccine will be available by December.

NHS staff will get priority, followed by those who live in care homes and everybody over eighty until it will be the turn of those over seventy-five and below.

Health officials are really enthusiastic about this latest development and, what's more, Oxford, too, continues its efforts to get a vaccine ready as soon as possible.

Do we dare to hope that this is the beginning of the end?

18th November

So, we are in lockdown again. Fewer people in the street and on the bus, the majority of shops and stores closed, with the exception of some cafés and bars who offer a takeaway service.

Marks &Spencer has kept its doors open, but only on the ground floor from where we can reach the groceries in the basement. The upper floor remains closed.

There are little or no Christmas decorations in the high street and little sign of any pre-Christmas activity.

It's a sober picture that lends itself to the onlooker and does not allow for any sense of festivity to be felt.

As yet, nobody really knows what Christmas will bring this year and any plans are up in the air. All will depend on the kind of restrictions that will be implemented.

We hear that an American firm called 'Moderna' has also developed a vaccine that will be ninety-five percent effective. But it will take until 2021 before it will be widely available.

First, we have to get through the winter.

25th November

At this time of year, everybody wants to begin preparations for Christmas but, with the lockdown still in place, this has become quite impossible.

Everybody's question is: 'What will happen when the lockdown comes to an end on 2nd December?'

Finally, the government has spoken after having discussed the matter thoroughly with the four countries of the UK.

Restrictions will ease for five days only, from 23rd to 27th December. Up to three households are allowed to meet but not in pubs or restaurants.

Travel restrictions will ease as well. Travellers coming to the UK can shorten their quarantine by having the test.

They must, however, pay for this test as it is not provided by the NHS. It will cost £120 or £200 which might put some people off from travelling at all.

29th November

From among the seven vaccines which are being developed, the UK has invested in the three major ones:

Pfizer with ninety percent efficiency, Moderna is very similar, and the Oxford vaccine AstraZeneca is sixty-two percent effective after the first vaccination and, when given two full doses, up to ninety percent.

The government reckons that the population could be vaccinated by the end of next spring.

Meanwhile, it is said that some backbenchers find the strict measures of the highest tier in some parts of England unfair, and they are likely to be revised during the course of the following weeks.

They are meant to come into force on Wednesday after the lockdown has come to an end on Tuesday.

From Denmark, we hear of the strange story where millions of minks had to be destroyed on a mink farm when it was discovered that the animals had caught a mutated form of coronavirus.

1st December

These days, two-thirds of the news is about the coronavirus and its latest development. Today is the last day of the lockdown to be replaced tomorrow by the three-tier system.

Words like devastation, closures, going into administration, job losses, redundancies and poor sales figures are accompanied by the implications these have on people's morale and mental condition.

Therefore, we hear again and again about worry and anxiety among people which then leads to depression and/or alcoholism. More children are being abused online. It all is a very bleak beginning of winter.

Debenhams, which has been in existence for two hundred and forty-two years is going into administration, followed by Acadia which owns Dorothy Perkins and Top Shop, which means thirteen thousand and twelve thousand job losses respectively.

It is all too obvious in the high street: shops have closed for good and shop fronts are being barricaded.

And, among all this, the market for Christmas trees is having a bumper year!

2nd December

Among all the gloomy news we have been getting, it is a real spark of hope to hear that the UK is the very first country in the world to make the vaccine available. It is the particular vaccine that was developed by Pfizer and has to be transported at -70 degrees Celsius.

Vaccinations are getting ready to start next week and, in this way, a civilian project is being activated of such large proportions as it has never been seen before. This is an absolute first!

The residents in nursing homes will be the first to be vaccinated, followed closely by the staff of the NHS and those over eighty.

"This is the beginning of the end," we hear Matt Hancock say and he is optimistic that, come spring, most of the population will have had their first vaccination and people will be able to return to a more normal life.

It is not quite known yet how long the immunisation will last, but we can truly say that something which normally takes years to develop has been achieved in eight months.

An outstanding feat on the scientific front!

4th December

The news is telling us that the whole campaign of vaccination will start tomorrow, the extent of which is quite unprecedented in the history of this country, and even around the world.

It will take many months and the authorities warn us that nothing will change for the time being and that we still must continue to be watchful and on-guard against catching this deadly disease.

At the same time, however, with this vaccination programme there is new hope entering the equation, and perhaps, by Easter next year, we will be in a much better position than we are now.

We can then focus on getting the economy going again which has suffered enormous losses, not only in this country but worldwide. There is hardly any sector that is not affected by its downturn.

As for the immediate future, I am sure, everybody will make use of the permission to be with family and to celebrate Christmas in its usual joyful manner.

8th December

A ninety-year-old British woman is the first in the world to be vaccinated against COVID-19.

As this vaccine has to be stored at -70 degrees Celsius, it is predominantly kept in certain hospitals all over the country.

While the good news of these first vaccinations and a second one in three weeks' time is reaching the public, it gives everybody the uplifting feeling that a way out of this dilemma is in sight.

This Pfizer vaccine which is, at the moment, the only one ready to be used will be followed by the Moderna and the Oxford vaccine by the end of the year.

The Oxford vaccine, in particular, will be much easier to transport and will be cheaper too.

This latest development presents such a milestone that it will be remembered for a long time to come.

Perhaps this is the best and greatest gift that the whole nation has received this winter, in time for Christmas!

13th December

Panto groups are taking to the streets to entertain the local residents. Standing on their doorsteps, they can listen to the popular tunes of Mary Poppins, or some other popular solos sung by the artists.

"It's been hard," they say, "but we are determined to survive." In London, some performances are taking place, in the Palladium, for instance, but the majority of pantos have been cancelled.

London is presently under tier two but, because the number of cases is still rising, this will be reviewed next week.

Meanwhile, the rule of three households to meet over Christmas still stands in order to allow families to get together.

The shops are open to catch up with some of the Christmas trade offering some fantastic bargains, particularly in clothing.

Times are still hard but, generally, the mood has become one of anticipation and good cheer.

14th December

Vaccinations have begun in many parts of the country. Despite this, London will be moved into tier three as of Wednesday.

Cases are rising at an alarming speed in London and Essex, and Matt Hancock speaks of a new variant of the virus which, however, does not make you in any way more ill and will respond to the vaccine.

All this throws a shadow over the Christmas period. Up till now, it still stands that three households are allowed to come together. Will this continue to be the case, or must we be prepared for a last-minute change?

Businesswise, the new restrictions in the Southeast are a blow to the expected Christmas trade, in shops as well as in the hospitality sector when pubs, bars cafés and restaurants are only allowed a takeaway service.

It is extremely hard for some of us and yet, people do speak about the beginning of the end of this crisis.

17th December

The rapid rise of cases in the Southeast has put pressure on the Prime Minister with regard to a relaxation of rules over the Christmas period.

He is addressing the public in a press conference saying that it would be "inhuman" to prevent people from coming together at Christmas.

So, the rule of three households being allowed to meet over Christmas between the 23rd and 27th December still stands, but he also added that people should take every care and "have yourself a little Christmas" this year, with the emphasis on "little".

People will have to apply their own judgement on whether to cancel their plans or to go ahead with them.

In many cases, families haven't been able to see each other for many months and are, therefore, looking forward to a small family gathering in order to see grandchildren and/or sons and daughters.

20th December

These are strange times, and it is going to be a Christmas like no other.

Since midnight last night, London has been put into tier four which means that all non-essential shops have to close, and it is advised not to travel in and out of London.

The reason for this change in restrictions is the new variant of the disease that is taking over the country.

In tiers two and three, only two households are now allowed to meet, and it applies for Christmas Day only.

In a press conference, the Prime Minister has addressed the nation by saying that he has no choice but to increase the restrictions since it is his task as Prime Minister to protect the nation and also the NHS which, presently, is in many areas at breaking point already.

For many this means, however, that Christmas plans will have to be scrapped and, for many elderly family members, it means that they will be spending Christmas alone at home.

22ⁿᵈ December

The coronavirus has reached Antarctica which, until now, had been free of the virus. Now, all seven continents are affected by it.

Closer to home, more than one thousand five hundred lorry drivers are stuck in Kent because France has closed its borders for fear of the new variant which can now be found in many parts of the UK.

Most likely, it came to our shores from abroad. This new spike in cases can potentially put the NHS under pressure if we are not able to curb it.

The R-number has moved above zero and is presently between 1.2 and 1.4 which is telling us that this new variant is spreading significantly.

Many countries have cancelled any flights from the UK leaving many people stranded when they had hoped to be home for Christmas.

It, therefore, looks like we have to make the best of a bad situation.

For many people, this means making sacrifices and putting one's hope in the foreseeable future.

26th December

Christmas has come and gone. It is very quiet in London. The streets are, again, deserted.

But Christmas Day was a cold and sunny day and people were able to go for walks. People could be in touch with those close to them either by video calls or Skype.

From South Africa came the news about yet another mutation of the virus and, so, all flights to and from that part of the world have been cancelled.

Those who wanted to travel over Christmas were equally disappointed as flights from the UK are, at least for the time being, an absolute no-no.

Lucky were those who could at least spend Christmas Day together or else could welcome a visitor from their support bubble. This last possibility is unchanged.

But it was altogether an opportunity to let the spirit of Christmas be among us despite all obstacles and restrictions.

30th December

There is little change on the horizon. Cases continue to rise just about everywhere.

There is now a shortage of intensive care beds. People with the virus are being treated in an ambulance while waiting to be admitted to the A&E department.

At present, the number of cases in hospitals has overtaken the number of cases when they peaked in April.

But there is light at the end of the tunnel. The Oxford vaccine by AstraZeneca has now been approved by the medical regulators.

This vaccine does not require to be kept at very low temperatures like the Pfizer vaccine but can simply be kept in the fridge.

The UK has ordered a hundred million ampoules and they will be in circulation as early as next week. The vaccination programme can begin in earnest!

2nd January 2021

New Year arrived in a quiet and somewhat subdued way. People were asked to take the regulations seriously and not to go to New Year's parties but to stay at home.

And people did, apart from the usual exceptions where the existing order is ignored, and people follow their own inclinations.

The travel ban to and from Great Britain continues, and most of England is now in tier four.

So far, there is no improvement in the situation. Cases are still on the up and hospitals all over the country find it difficult to cope.

The streets continue to be very quiet and not many people are out and about. It is difficult to comprehend that, in spite of all these precautions, numbers are not coming down.

Has it got to do with the mutated virus which, they say, is even more infectious than the previous one?

We certainly haven't seen the last of it yet!

5th January

The situation continues to be dire. The Prime Minister has announced that a third lockdown will be implemented as of Thursday.

Cases of the new variant are increasing at an alarming rate and, though, for the moment, there are enough beds available in the NHS, there aren't enough doctors and nurses to deal with the large number of patients. They are being stretched to the limit, and nurses admit that, after a ten-hour shift, they often come home crying from exhaustion.

The number of admissions is now higher than it was in March or April last year when we thought we had reached the peak.

And, so, the message from the Prime Minister is again: 'stay at home, protect the NHS and save lives!'

A glimmer of hope that he has given us is the fact that both vaccines, the Pfizer and the AstraZeneca, are being rolled out in a big way and he hopes that, by mid-February, most people of eighty or over will have had their first vaccination.

6th January

The biggest vaccination programme this country has ever seen is underway. So far, the Prime Minister tells us in a press conference, that one point three million people have received their first jab.

As figures show, one million people are affected by the virus. He said the government will give daily updates about the vaccination rollout.

This comes as the UK recorded—for the first time during the pandemic—more than sixty thousand confirmed positive COVID-19 tests in one day, and eight hundred and thirty deaths occurred within twenty-eight days of a positive test.

People are naturally concerned about how they will cope mentally with yet another lockdown.

A woman said very wisely: "I'll relax without feeling guilty." Other people may well discover the benefits which a discipline like yoga or meditation can bring.

They provide a healthy sort of energy, and feelings of loneliness may well be kept in check.

11th January

The UK is facing the most difficult phase of the pandemic right now. At least these are the latest words of the experts.

The mayor of London has declared a 'difficult incident' as London hospitals are threatened to be overwhelmed. There were more than a thousand deaths in four days running.

A mammoth effort is being made to stick to the huge vaccination rollout.

Seven new hubs or centres have been put up in the Southeast, and it is the government's aim to have fifteen million people vaccinated by mid-February, among them are care homes, vulnerable people, NHS staff and the over seventies.

Hospitals, surgeries and, eventually, many pharmacies will be engaged in this programme.

While this is going on, there are still those who flock in front of the surrounding hospitals shouting that it is nothing but a hoax and that hospitals are really quite empty.

It is hard to believe!

15th January

Students at a secondary school in London had the idea to deliver some pizzas to the nursing staff of a London hospital.

It was a surprising and welcome gift for those who had been so busy on their shift that they had hardly any time for a quick meal.

One nurse who was at the end of her ten-hour shift actually burst into tears at the sight of the pizzas. Such a friendly gesture is greatly appreciated under such circumstances.

But the opposite is true too.

It has become a problem for nurses of the NHS to deal with all the hate mail in which the denial of the disease has taken on an aggressive and hostile stance.

Meanwhile, there are the first signs in the Southeast and London that the restrictions of the latest lockdown are beginning to work, but it is by far too early to be certain about it.

Because of a new variant discovered in Brazil, the government has put a ban on all flights from South America and also Portugal.

And so, the battle continues.

17th January

A new person with COVID-19 is admitted to hospital every thirty seconds, a survey has shown. There is a flood of patients coming in all the time and the work required is relentless.

The good news, however, is that there are now more people being vaccinated than there are people falling ill.

As of Monday, there will be ten more big vaccination centres opening up in different places of the country. So far, three point five million have received their first dose, and some have already had their second one.

Apart from the Pfizer and AstraZeneca vaccines, there is now the Moderna vaccine.

But scientists say that, despite our efforts to get people vaccinated, we will have to face tough weeks ahead before things can finally begin to improve, and the NHS will remain under immense pressure to cope with the influx of patients.

21st January

The medical staff in hospitals around England agree that they are now facing a situation that is far surpassing the conditions as they applied to last April.

This includes that there are fifty percent more patients and the death rate is at a record high. There were more than one thousand eight hundred dead during the last twenty-four hours. It is a race against time.

It has been reported that, at the beginning of this lockdown, the rise in cases was phenomenal and, according to public opinion, it will take weeks before we begin to notice the benefits of the vaccinations.

Sixty-five more vaccination centres have been made available in England, including a mosque and a Sikh temple, and there are many pharmacies and surgeries now that offer their services.

All in all, the figures show that four million eight hundred thousand people have had their first vaccination, and the government is confident that they can hit the target of fifteen million by mid-February.

23rd January

On 23rd January last year, the Chinese authorities severed transport links out of Wuhan and confined the population to their homes. Wuhan has long since recovered from the world's first outbreak of Covid-19.

Its streets are bustling again.

As for the rest of the world, however, the situation is less optimistic, and medical teams, ministers, prime ministers and presidents struggle to keep up with demands on the various vaccines which are now in operation.

Shortages of the Pfizer vaccine has stalled the vaccination programme in the EU, while the UK has still got enough supply to work toward its target of mid-February.

The new President of America, Joe Biden, has initiated a nationwide programme, saying that half a million lives have already been lost to the disease.

26th January

More than one hundred thousand lives have been claimed so far, and the scientists warn that the number of deaths will only come down very slowly.

On the positive side, however, one in every eight people has been vaccinated, in total seven million and, as more and more centres are being made available, this trend will continue.

The number of deaths worldwide stands at two million and it will take us well into February before we will notice any difference in the spread of the disease.

The Prime Minister in his press conference today expressed his sorrow about so many lives lost and he pledged that lessons will be learnt for future epidemics.

But the truth is that we are faced here with a virus the strength of which has never been experienced before, and it is causing a world crisis the scale of which has not been witnessed since the Second World War.

1st February

The new South African variant has found its way into our country now, and testing is available to those who are affected by it.

The question arose whether the various vaccines would be effective as a protection against this new variant. But those fears could be laid to rest by the scientists.

Both the Pfizer and the AstraZeneca vaccines offer sufficient protection against the virus in their different forms.

On a brighter note, it can now be stated that all care home residents have been offered the first jab, and the Prime Minister commented by saying that this was a "crucial milestone".

Until now, nine million people have received their first vaccination, and half a million have already had their second one.

But caution is still expected of us, and all the rules are still in place and have to be followed. This virus will still be with us for a good while to come.

3rd February

Captain Sir Tom Moore, the veteran who raised £33 million for the NHS by continuing to walk a hundred laps in his own backyard in Bedfordshire and who was subsequently knighted by the Queen, fell ill with COVID-19 and was admitted to hospital, where he died being one hundred years old.

His daughter was by his bedside and a second daughter was present on Zoom.

His memory will live on and has already inspired young and old to overcome physical ailments and to walk a certain mileage in order to raise more money for various charities.

Meanwhile, the fight goes on even though it seems as if we have finally reached the peak of hospital admissions and deaths.

But it is a very slow decline, especially since this new South African variant poses a renewed threat, and scientists are very vigilant about this new development.

10th February

As of next week, stricter rules about border control will be implemented.

Travellers to the UK and Ireland will have to isolate for ten days. They have to stay in a hotel especially assigned to cater for such travellers, and they have to pay £1,750 for this stay, to cover the costs.

Failing to isolate will result in a fine of £1,000.

This rule will apply to people who arrive here from one of the countries which are on the red list.

Failing to declare the country from which they come or return to or lying about it, will end in the payment of £10,000.

These extremely strict rules are meant to prevent any new variants, including the South African one, to enter this country.

The latter was so far found in a limited number of cases, one hundred and forty-seven cases to be precise, and it seems unlikely that it will overrun the current variant in England, which is the Kent variant, as measures have been put in place to prevent it from spreading any further.

11th February

Yesterday a year ago, the first case of coronavirus was discovered in Wuhan in China, and the first case in England followed when a lady returned from China and was admitted to hospital.

Since then, two hundred and sixty million cases have been registered worldwide, together with two point five million deaths.

It is a pandemic the likes of which we have never witnessed before, and it has left the whole world in a deplorable state.

Now a team of WHO was allocated to China to investigate more closely the actual origin of the disease.

It is, they say, unlikely that the source of the virus originated in a laboratory, but more research is needed to get more precise information about it.

It has been suggested that it was some live animals sold in the market which first transmitted the virus to humans.

Scientists wonder whether it is here to stay like the flu virus, and will we have to be vaccinated against it on a regular basis?

15th February

The target has been reached: fifteen million people—the over 70s, NHS staff and home residents and their staff as well as the clinically vulnerable—have been vaccinated.

Astonishingly, this implies that one in four people had their first jab. But this is no time to slow down.

The next step on the list is the over sixties, and the second vaccination will be due for many people in March. Results begin to show.

Admissions to hospitals have come down significantly, but the number is, at present, still higher than it was in April last year.

Deaths have come down as well, particularly in the older population, which is an encouraging sign.

As of today, the rule to isolate in a hotel if you arrive from a country on the red list comes into action. As the Prime Minister said, the lifting of the current measures will be "cautious, but irreversible", in other words: no further lockdown!

It seems we are yet a long way off from any normal lifestyle!

19th February

A global effort is being made to provide all poorer countries with the different kinds of vaccines which are now on the market.

The cheapest vaccine which is also easy to travel is the AstraZeneca. Moderna and Pfizer are more expensive and difficult to store at -70 degrees.

Ahead of the meeting of the G7 in Cornwall, the Prime Minister pledged that all surplus vaccines will be given to countries less fortunate than us. As the UK ordered more than four hundred million, there will be some leftover even when everyone has been vaccinated twice.

It is of utmost importance that every country around the world will have the necessary means to vaccinate their population, for:

"Nobody is safe until everybody is safe."

If we want to eradicate this virus, we must all join together and make sure that we share our resources.

The last time we succeeded in suppressing a potentially deadly illness was when smallpox became a thing of the past.

23rd February

The Prime Minister has laid out his road map for the recovery of our country.

The gradual lifting of the lockdown will proceed in four steps starting on the 8th of March, when children will return to school, and it will stretch over the period of three months until the 21st of June, when he hopes that all restrictions can finally be abandoned.

We will have to wait for another six weeks before all shops will open again on the 12th of April.

This kind of cautious withdrawal of restrictions is what he meant when he said that lifting of restrictions will be "cautious, but irreversible."

In the meantime, the vaccination rollout is proving a real success.

Both the Pfizer and AstraZeneca vaccines offer ninety percent immunity, even among the older generation, and the hope is that, thanks to the vaccinations, we will finally get on top of the virus and of any mutation that might yet occur.

24th February

What made the second and third lockdown more difficult than the first one is the fact that during the long waiting time where we had hoped that something would happen, nothing did happen.

But now, the general feeling has changed. As soon as the four steps leading us out of the lockdown have become common knowledge, a new sense of vitality has made itself felt.

With this roadmap given by the Prime Minister, people are beginning to see that the end is in sight.

The 12th of April is important as this is the date when shops, hairdressers and beauty salons will reopen.

By the end of May, people can receive friends and family indoors.

And there is the 21st of June, when, hopefully, we can return to something resembling normality. These dates have given people an incentive, a goal to aim for.

Meanwhile, the new President of America has paid tribute to America's half a million deaths, so far, the highest number registered in the world.

26th February

The alert level has now come down from level five to level four.

Matt Hancock, in his press conference, gave us some more news about the current situation.

The good news is that, yes, numbers in hospitals are declining and that, yes, the number of deaths are falling. There is a 'but', however.

Don't be fooled by this. There are still fifteen thousand people being treated in hospital which is far too many, and there are still three hundred people dying every day, again, a number which is far too high.

And, at the same time, there are regions in the UK where cases are rising again. The battle is not yet won, and it would be a mistake to relax now when we are so close.

'Don't wreck it now,' is his warning.

At the same time, he stressed that the vaccination rollout continues at great speed. So far, there are nineteen million people who have had their first jab.

3rd March

The time of the first lockdown went by reasonably quickly.

It was still a novelty then and could, with some sense of the unexpected, be turned round to one's advantage. We discovered new aspects in ourselves by spending more time on new projects like gardening, baking, cooking new recipes, painting or spending time with the family—all in all, it might be said that it unleashed creative energies in us which may normally lie dormant.

We began to think laterally.

The second lockdown and, then the third, on the contrary, had the taste of the déjà vu, and the attitude changed from embracing it to loathing it.

It quite literally seemed to last forever. People were growing tired of having their liberty cut in such a drastic way. The cold and unfriendly weather also played its part: nowhere to go, even a walk in these weather conditions is not a welcome exercise; everything is shut; being at home became a tiresome task that seemed to paralyse the energies.

The Prime Minister gave us new hope by outlining his roadmap for the next three months and, with it, a possible change was finally in sight.

8th March

"Today is the first step toward a sense of normality," was the Prime Minister's comment when all children returned to school. The plan is that they will be equipped with rapid testing kits for themselves and their parents.

More people are also allowed to meet outdoors, but the real change will come when indoor visits are allowed again, which won't be before the 17th of May.

This very gradual, step-by-step removal of restrictions is the safest way to avoid another major surge of the virus, and people are asked to keep this in mind.

The Nightingale Hospitals have now been closed as there is no need for them anymore, with numbers still falling and the NHS being in a position where they can cope with the number of cases being admitted.

To mention is also that Ghana is the first country in Africa that has been provided with a vaccine.

11th March

The future of the London Zoo has become uncertain.

It has missed out of the millions of visitors who visit each year, and for the running of the zoo and the maintenance of the animals' welfare, the zoo depends entirely on their contributions.

The pandemic leaves many more victims in its wake.

By the time it is over, the high street will have undergone significant changes. Big department stores will be no more.

There is Debenhams which has closed its doors for good. John Lewis will have to downsize. Brands like Top Shop and others will change hands.

The theatre world lies in ruins and, unless they can open in summer and are allowed full capacity, they will not survive.

The airline industry has suffered greatly.

So, a lot will depend on whether or not the prediction about 21st June will indeed become a reality and many parts of our society will welcome it with a great sigh of relief.

20th March

There is a lot of controversy going on in Europe concerning the efficacy of the AstraZeneca vaccine.

It has disrupted the vaccination rollout in Europe to a very large extent. Vaccination centres stand empty and idle with nobody there.

However, the regulators both in the UK and in the EU maintain that it is safe and getting vaccinated is still the best option by far.

It is said that the AstraZeneca vaccine could cause blood clots in the brain of some people.

The UK has responded to this claim by saying that it is extraordinarily rare, and here the vaccination programme continues to be very strong indeed.

Up to recent figures, more than twenty-six million people have received their jab and the government hopes that every adult will have received their first jab by July.

Due to the delay in manufacturing the AstraZeneca vaccine in India, there won't be any first vaccinations in April, but the second dose will continue to be administered throughout.

23rd March

It's been a year today since the first lockdown.

The Queen reflected on the grief and loss of the one hundred and twenty-six thousand who died because of COVID-19.

At eight o'clock in the evening, candles were lit everywhere, and a candle burnt in front of number ten.

The landmarks of London were lit with a yellow light to remember all those who died, and a moment of silence was being observed.

Boris Johnson warned that a new wave, which is present in most European countries, "might well wash up on our shores".

The dispute about AstraZeneca and its supplies is still ongoing in Europe.

Despite all this, the vaccination rollout continues in this country.

The number of vaccinated people has risen to twenty-eight million.

There is no doubt there is a more optimistic mood in England, and people are eagerly awaiting the 12th of April when shops will be open again. Easter is more likely to be another quiet affair though.

24th March

One man's loss is another man's gain.

It is reported that the DIY stores have seen a sharp rise in sales. Houseplants, too, have been bought more readily in comparison to recent years.

It does seem that the lockdowns we have experienced helped us to change our habits and, in many cases, we turned into homemakers.

We were and are forced to look for alternatives.

Our focus has shifted. Whereas before we looked elsewhere for distractions and spent our free time going out and taking advantage of what was on offer in terms of having a good time, we now seem to have found a new way of thinking, telling us what is really important and essential.

Being at home has found a new way of appreciation.

Is it indeed possible that our values have shifted? And modern technology has come into its own, at the same time, giving us the chance to get in touch.

29th March

Travel restrictions have been eased over the Easter holidays, and up to six people or two households are able to meet outdoors.

It is being stressed that the danger of catching the virus is much greater indoors than it is in the open air.

Caution is the word that the Prime Minister has used repeatedly in today's press conference, but he also encouraged people to enjoy the sunshine and do more exercising, as outdoor sports like tennis or cricket are now also within the limits of what is allowed.

While Europe is going through a third wave, the death rate and admissions in this country keep on coming down.

However, the threat from Europe is real and might well be felt over here sooner or later.

So, the message is: enjoyment, yes, but we also have to remain vigilant and aware of the fact that COVID-19 is still very much part of our lives.

12th April

The second step of our "road map to freedom" has been taken. Today, all non-essential shops, including beauty salons and hairdressers, opened their doors again.

Pubs, cafés and restaurants are allowed to serve food and drink, but it has to be outdoors. The high street was a lot livelier compared to the previous three months when it appeared to be a ghost town.

People were queuing early in the morning to be the first to get into the shops, especially shops that sell sportswear.

Everybody is hoping that this reopening will make up for the quiet weeks and months which seem to be finally behind us now. It does look as if people are ready to spend money again, after the savings we made during the lockdown.

But it is also obvious that, in every high street, we can see the remnants of closures, a reminder of those who did not survive this difficult and harassing time.

So, let us hope that this "road map to freedom" will indeed be a step in the right direction and that, this time, it will be "irreversible", to repeat the Prime Minister's own words.

17th April

A new heavy wave of coronavirus is sweeping through India, and scientists are studying the new virus in order to establish whether it could diminish the effectiveness of the various vaccines.

The worldwide total of deaths has surpassed four million and, in different parts of the world, no real abatement can be seen which would indicate that the virus is retreating.

In England, however, the situation is more hopeful, and people take tentative steps to move around a bit more freely.

With the weather being warm and sunny, those restaurants and cafés in the high street which have outdoor seating, see an influx of customers which gives the street a Mediterranean feel.

Today, we also witnessed the funeral of the Duke of Edinburgh which took place in the chapel of Windsor Castle. It was a very elegant but simple affair, with only the closest family being present.

The Queen, face mask on, her head bowed, sat alone, and everybody who has lost loved ones during COVID-19 could feel her grief and was able to share it with her.

24th April

India has now been put on the red list.

Only residents from the UK are allowed in and have to stay in one of the allocated hotels at their own cost. They have to stay in quarantine for ten days before they are allowed to travel to their destination.

India has now the highest death rate worldwide.

The hospitals are completely overrun and cannot cope with the number of patients. People are lying on makeshift beds in the corridors waiting to be treated. Ventilators are in short supply, and the UK has stepped in by sending a shipment that is so urgently needed.

At the other end of the stick, is Israel: for the first time, there are no deaths reported. Vaccination has been rolled out at a fantastic rate, with the result, that the country is as good as free of the coronavirus.

The UK has advanced at a slightly slower pace but the lockdown, combined with the large number of vaccinations, is having a positive result.

Do we dare to expect a more normal way of life in the near future?

30th April

Twenty-two million people in the UK live in an area where there are no COVID-19 deaths.

At the same time, vaccinations continue, this time it's the turn of the forty to forty-five-year-olds who are asked to come forward.

In India, the situation has become desperate, not only in the big cities but also in rural areas.

There were three hundred thousand deaths in the last week alone.

Hospitals cannot take in any more patients. People are dying in the streets, and it is hard to keep up with burying the dead.

Right now, India has the highest death rate ever recorded, even higher than Brazil.

It is partly due to a new variant which has mainly been discovered in some of the towns. New Delhi and Mumbai are especially hard hit and find it impossible to cope with the large numbers. A vaccination programme has begun but is proceeding rather slowly.

Meanwhile, people are left to die.

1st May

We have all been affected by this pandemic, every one of us, be it financially, mentally or physically.

We had to give up our social habits and be content with staying at home. We knew that we had to quarantine when we had to go abroad as so many business people will know.

Life must go on, but it has taken a different route, creating a different atmosphere among people.

For some of us, this meant that we became more conscious of our pattern of behaviour and could then see the chance to alter or improve it.

Maybe we changed our attitude towards ourselves and/or towards others and, by doing so, we learnt that nothing is permanent, everything fluctuates and eventually changes.

That implies that we can view the outcome of a difficult situation in a different light. But there are also those who, in view of such obstacles which we have to face, become annoyed, resentful or angry. Like everything which occurs in the course of our life, we are always given a choice when faced with a new situation.

Those of us who proved to be resourceful, have gained rather than lost.

12th May

There is still much talk about a "new normal". Perhaps we should ask ourselves the question: what is normal, and what do we refer to when we speak of the "new normal"? Perhaps normal is simply what we are used to and what we took for granted when we lived our daily lives. We value our freedom and, so, if we are prevented from doing what we have always been doing, we are not sure anymore where we stand.

Living with lockdown is certainly part of this "new normal" which takes some getting used to and, of course, we don't want to be inconvenienced for more than is necessary.

As of Monday, the 17^{th of} May, we are allowed to meet indoors again, and we can even hug our nearest and dearest. So, at least our gestures that express affection and love have not changed but were simply suspended for a while.

But can this experience with the pandemic change us in a way that will be a lasting change? Are we perhaps learning that we are not only separate entities? Such insight can then lead to the notion that we are really meant to live peacefully with one another.

The news, however, tells us differently. The human mind has an extraordinary ability to adapt, but also to forget easily. I think many people will, once the lockdown restrictions have been lifted, return to the same habits, the same plans and desires, needs and contradictions as before.

But some will have given it all some more serious thought and an inward change will have taken place which will stay with them.

17th May

Many people felt excited and happy because, from today, we can not only meet our friends and family indoors, but we can also have a meal out in a pub or restaurant without having to sit outside in the chill of the evening.

However, the Prime Minister warned that, as we have reached this new target of our road map, we are meant to proceed with great caution.

Some believe that restrictions are coming off too soon and too fast and, not only that, but the threat which now comes from the Delta variant first discovered in India is real.

At the moment, it seems to be mainly concentrated in Bolton and whereabouts.

It is said that this variant which has caused so much havoc in India is more transmissible than the so-called Kent variant, the virus we have had so far in the UK.

People who live in the area of Bolton are asked to come forward to get vaccinated. It seems to be now a race between this new intruder and the vaccinations.

That is why people are asked to take great care when they follow the new rules of their regained freedom.

28th May

Because of the pandemic, there is now a huge backlog of untreated patients in the NHS.

Five million non-urgent operations have to be dealt with and, with a shortage of doctors, it is quite problematic to begin to minimise the impact this has on people's lives.

Dentists, too, are facing a long waiting list and some patients have been asked to wait for two years or longer.

But not all is bad news. The number of cases is still coming down and the country is, at last, enjoying some degree of freedom which goes down well with everybody.

However, seventy-five percent of cases are now due to the Indian variant, and it is particularly prominent in certain areas of England. The advice is, therefore, not to travel to or from these affected areas.

People are asked to be especially mindful of the virus.

That is why the Prime Minister has withheld his decision on whether or not the last step of the road map is going to be implemented on 21st June and urges people to come forward in order to get vaccinated.

1st June

For the first time since March 2020, the UK government did not announce any new deaths caused by the virus.

The death rate has been falling steadily since its peak back in January. Even keeping in mind that the figures are often lower right at the start of the week, it is still a significant moment in the development of the disease.

In stark contrast, Peru's death rate has doubled in recent days, and it is now higher than in Brazil. One hundred and eighty thousand people are known to have died.

But there is also the story of a small town in Brazil—Serrano—which has a population of forty-five thousand.

Nearly all the adults have been vaccinated in an experiment that wants to find out how far mass vaccination can stop the spread of the virus. Findings suggest that the virus can be controlled after seventy five percent of the population has been dosed twice. It proved to be successful in Serrano.

This gives rise to the hope that we will eventually reach the point when we can begin to be free of COVID-19.

7th June

The G7 meeting will be taking place in Cornwall where donations to the developing countries will also be discussed.

Boris Johnson wants to push the vaccination programme by saying that he wants the rest of the world to be vaccinated by the end of 2022.

It is a keen undertaking and some countries have already made it clear exactly how many vaccines they intend to donate.

The other big topic will, of course, be climate change and, with America being back in the game under the leadership of Joe Biden, the meeting stands a good chance to be successful, as the ministers and leaders unite under the rule of a common aim which is meant to build a better and healthier world.

What is required is a lot of prudence, foresight and firm commitment if they want to stand by certain conditions, and, who knows, it may eventually lead to a more peaceful world where tolerance and mutual acceptance are the cornerstones.

8th June

The Greek islands are serenading again.

The Greek government has prioritised the islands to get their local population vaccinated in order to be able to open their doors to prospective tourists.

But, for the time being, it is all a bit uncertain and up in the air. Bakers and butchers are not sure at all how many they should cater for.

True, there are some German and French tourists arriving on Milos, but the British tourists are still few and far between.

Thailand, too, is trying to open up the tourist market after a year of closure.

Again, it means to get people vaccinated as soon as possible but, like so many countries, Thailand finds it hard to get hold of enough vaccines even though they produce their own AstraZeneca.

11th June

In the course of next year, the UK will donate more than a hundred million surplus vaccines to poorer countries, already starting in the coming weeks and months, says the Prime Minister.

He is urging fellow G7 leaders to make similar pledges, ahead of the actual summit.

President Joe Biden is promising five hundred million Pfizer vaccine doses to ninety-two low or middle-income countries including the African Union.

As for the 21st of June, when the government intends to declare that the pandemic was officially over in England, it now seems more and more unlikely that this is going to happen following the rise of cases of the virus first discovered in India.

Ninety-one percent of cases in the UK are due to this variant now, and last week saw seven thousand new cases.

A decision will be made on 14th June.

14th June

We all heard the news today and, as many had already predicted, we are not going to have our "freedom day" on 21st June, at least not yet.

As the Prime Minister told us in his announcement today, it is better to be patient a little longer than to risk going backwards, and he reminded us that he wanted this roadmap to be irreversible.

As infections of the Delta virus are on the up, a new date has been given when all remaining restrictions will be withdrawn by the government.

It will now be on 19th July.

But the situation will be revised in two weeks' time. If the prospects are favourable, this date can be brought forward.

Meanwhile, the plan is to get another million people, aged eighteen and over, vaccinated. We are assured that the vaccinations are working and that they are beginning to prevent many people from getting seriously sick.

15th June

What was new in the Prime Minister's press conference yesterday was, above all, that he no longer speaks in terms of being free of the virus, but he now puts it that we have to learn to live with it.

What he is saying, in other words, is that there will continue to be cases of COVID-19, that they might even increase as we loosen the restrictions on 19th July, and that, sadly, a small number of people will still die, but steps will be taken to minimise its impact.

One important step is, of course, to get the population vaccinated as much as possible.

He is "confident", as he says, that this date of 19th July will be the day when we will take the final step on the road map, on the road to recovery.

This means, above all, that the rule of social distancing will be scrapped in public places like cinemas, theatres, pubs and restaurants for whom it is another blow that they have to wait for another month before they can finally allow their venues to be filled with people again and to earn that much-needed cash.

18th June

People aged eighteen and over will be invited to book their first jab in what the NHS is describing as a "watershed moment."

About one and a half million texts are to be sent to people aged eighteen and twenty today.

"Offering all adults a jab less than two hundred days after the programme was launched, is one of our country's greatest collective achievements," those were the words of the Prime Minister.

There was a tearful reunion when finally, after not having seen each other for one year, ninety-two-year-old twins, Minnie Welsh and Patrick Speed, could meet again.

They live in different units of the same care home. The pair is able to spend time together again after having received their COVID-19 vaccinations.

Mr Speed expressed it in the following words:

"We were born together, and we are back together."
Ms Welsh says the reunion left them "full of joy."

19th June

Last year, COVID-19 wiped out UK's summer music festival season and, this year, only a handful are taking place.

One such event is the Download Festival in Donnington Park in Leicester this coming weekend.

The Download Festival is, for the government, a test to assess how crowd events can be run safely. The audience will be smaller—only ten thousand people compared to one hundred and ten thousand in a normal year.

Everyone must provide proof of a negative COVID-19 test result in order to gain entrance and take a test after the festival.

Despite the rainy weather, Download devotees are glad to be able to return.

Amy Ford, who has been coming to this festival since 2014, says: "We needed to be back on the holy ground; it's where we belong."

20th June

Queues are forming outside pop-up vaccination centres across England.

Football grounds and parks are among the venues which are being used for this purpose.

It's the turn of the younger age groups. According to the latest figures, more than forty-four million people in the UK have had their first vaccination, and more than thirty-three million have had their second dose.

In contrast to the positive news here in the UK, we get the news coming from Brazil that death rates have passed half a million, the third highest in the world after the US and India. Intensive care units are currently running at full capacity as the country deals with a third wave of infections. Experts have warned that thousands more will die because of the slow rollout of vaccines and the approach of winter.

28th June

After having been cancelled last summer, Wimbledon is back.

But there is a difference. There is no queuing and camping outside the courts in order to get entry. Tickets are sold online which leaves some disappointed and some happy.

Once inside, capacity is reduced by fifty percent, at least to start off with, but it is hoped that, in the second week, restrictions will be reduced, and all seats can be occupied.

The Prime Minister confirmed that it looks very likely that all remaining restrictions will be lifted on 19th July, but not before.

According to this prediction, we can expect things to feel differently from this date onwards.

It is also hoped that five million more will be vaccinated between now and the 19th of July, in an attempt to defeat the Delta variant.

3rd July

With the arrival of July, everybody is looking forward to the 19th with a high degree of expectancy. Will the remaining restrictions really be lifted? But what about this wretched Delta variant that is still causing damage in people's lives?

At first glance, life looks a lot more relaxed now than it was a month ago. The Wembley Stadium was packed with forty thousand fans when England played against Germany in the delayed Euro 2020, and their win was celebrated everywhere, in pubs, in the streets or at home.

Wimbledon is in full swing again after last year's cancellation. The rows of spectators are back again, and every seat is taken. Hardly anyone is wearing a face mask.

This all sounds and looks very promising, except that there is also the fact that the Delta virus is indeed affecting more and more people in all parts of the country. But serious cases where people had to be admitted to hospital have remained low, probably thanks to the vaccination rollout. It is mostly young people who catch the virus now.

So, what can we expect on the 19th? Surely, some kind of caution is still required and, accordingly, social distancing and face masks may well stay with us for some time to come.

5th July

Another press conference from the Prime Minister. He indicated that we would go ahead and lift most restrictions on 19th July, but that this will only be confirmed, and the final decision will be made in a week's time.

What stood out today was his comment that we will move from the government's dictate to personal responsibility. Everyone will be asked to use their own judgement and discretion when or when not to wear a face covering or apply the rule of keeping a certain distance. It will become voluntary rather than mandatory.

Though, he said, cases are on the increase, it begs the question: when, if not now, are we ever going to take the necessary step and return to something resembling a normal way of life? Now, in summer, seems to be a more opportune moment to move forward. In autumn, with the winter season approaching, it would be far more difficult, as the NHS will then have to cope with the winter flu and other such ailments as well.

He added that this final step of the road map is only possible because the vaccination rollout has been and still is so successful, and he stressed, again, that we must learn to live with this virus, as it is not going away in a hurry.

We will hear more on 12th July.

13th July

Those of us who had hoped that from Monday next week, our lives would be again what they were before the virus struck, are going to be disappointed. Not much will have changed. The virus is still with us and is still claiming its victims every day.

The only thing which will be different is that we will have to decide for ourselves how far we will go to protect ourselves and others. There will be many who will say that we cannot do without face masks or social distancing yet, and will, therefore, continue to cover their faces in crowded indoor spaces such as trains and busses.

We also know that it does matter whether we are with someone who has been vaccinated or is unvaccinated. Somebody who has not had the vaccination can potentially pass the virus on, though he or she may not display any symptoms. True responsibility starts with that.

If there is something the pandemic has taught us, it is the thought that we are protecting others when we protect ourselves.

19th July

At midnight last night, people, mostly young people, flocked together to celebrate the unlocking of the remaining restrictions. Everyone was in a party mood where the only criterion was "to have a good time." As this took place outdoors, the risk of catching the virus was minimal. After all, this is meant to be "freedom day." But to call it "freedom" is misreading the reality of things.

COVID-19 has not left us and therefore the comment by the government to proceed slowly and cautiously. I think the majority of us thought some time ago that this day was meant to be the day when we were free of the virus at long last, free of the disease which had dominated us for a good sixteen months.

The actual reality, however, looks different. Our only real defence is that a large proportion of the population has been vaccinated and was better equipped to withstand infection.

Can we, therefore, say that the actual reality of the 19th of July is an anti-climax? Not quite. The situation as we face it now is not quite so grim and hopeless as it seemed to be on so many occasions during the past weeks and months.

Many people will decide, since it is now up to them, to continue to wear a face covering and observe social distancing. The fact that it is no longer mandatory will be of benefit to pubs, bars and restaurants. Night clubs will ask for proof of vaccination or a negative test.

Theatres will be filled again to full capacity, but some West End shows have already had to be cancelled because of staff members testing positive.

So, all in all, the world has changed little, even on this so-called "freedom day." However, it is far from being what it was before COVID-19 arrived on the scene. Before, we could feel free to travel to any destination as and when we wanted, we could get together, go out and be close to friends and family according to our plans and intentions. Socialising was all part of our daily lives.

Much more is required from us now. We have to make an informed choice, do so with caution and apply common sense. Many of us have actually learned to act responsibly knowing that our behaviour either hinders or encourages the spread of the disease.

Man had to do some growing up. He had to learn to adopt an attitude where vigilance, self-awareness and the language of the heart are at the forefront, knowing that anything less will not help the world to recover from the most devastating reality the world has ever known. In that way, we are the bearers of our own destiny.

It was and is like a rude awakening. We are led to believe that we are indeed the builders of this world, our planet. Unconscious action has to give way to conscious decisions.

Are we up to it?

May the torch of the delayed Olympics 2020, which are presently taking place in Tokyo, be a beacon of light for future days to come when the spirit of comradeship outlives hostility, antagonism and ego-centricity, and where the human race finally recognises that it is bonded together in a unique and extraordinary way, that we are indeed one extended family where any enemy is ultimately defeated by way of the strength that our combined effort can and will produce.

Our experience with this virus has provided us with glimpses of such a vision which might one day become reality if and when we have learned that warfare is not the answer to all our problems, but that many problems arise because we fail to see that there is always an alternative, another way of seeing things and dealing with situations. In a way, it means breaking with a past where warfare was considered to be the only way out. The world had to deal with aggressors which are always opposed to a peaceful existence. It is their radical power struggle, their inhuman ambitions which can plunge us into a world of suffering and death. So perhaps, by having to cope with this aggressive disease which has cost us so many lives, the message that it brings is that here is a chance to conquer something that wants to be conquered, for the threat is not us, country against country, but that there is an aggressor that needs our full co-operation as human beings.